POLITICS AND SOCIETY IN ATHLONE, 1830–1885
A Rotten Borough

Maynooth Studies in Local History

GENERAL EDITOR Raymond Gillespie

This pamphlet is one of eight new additions to the Maynooth Studies in Local History series in 1999. Like their twenty predecessors, most are based on theses submitted for the M.A. in Local History at National University of Ireland, Maynooth. The pamphlets are not concerned primarily with the portrayal of the history of 'particular places'. All are local in their focus but that localisation is determined not by administrative boundaries but rather the limits of the experience of everyday life in the regions of Ireland over time. In some of these works the local experience is of a single individual while in others social, occupational or religious groups form the primary focus of enquiry.

The results of these enquiries into the shaping of local societies in the past emphasises, again, the diversity of the Irish historical experience. Ranging across problems of economic disaster, political transformation, rural unrest and religious tension, these works show how such problems were grounded in the realities of everyday life in local communities. The responses to such challenges varied from region to region, each place coping with problems in its own way, determined by its historical evolution and contemporary constraints.

The result of such investigations can only increase our awareness of the complexity of Ireland's historical evolution. Each work, in its own right, is also a significant contribution to our understanding of how specific Irish communities have developed in all their richness and diversity. In all, they demonstrate the vibrancy and challenging nature of local history.

Maynooth Studies in Local History: Number 26

POLITICS AND SOCIETY IN ATHLONE
1830–1885

A Rotten Borough

Jim Lenehan

IRISH ACADEMIC PRESS

DUBLIN • PORTLAND, OR

First published in 1999 by
IRISH ACADEMIC PRESS
44, Northumberland Road, Dublin 4, Ireland
and in the United States of America by
IRISH ACADEMIC PRESS
c/o ISBS, 5804 NE Hassalo Street, Portland, OR 97213.

website: www.iap.ie

British Library Cataloguing in Publication Data
Lenehen, Jimmy
  Politics and Society in Athlone, 1830–1885: A Rotten Borough
  1. Elections – Ireland – Athlone – History 2. Athlone (Ireland) – Social conditions
  – 19th century 3. Athlone (Ireland) – Politics and government – 19th century
  I. Title
  324.9'41815'081
  ISBN 071652676X

Library of Congress Cataloging-in-Publication Data
Lenehan, Jim.
    Politics and Society in Athlone, 1830–1885: A Rotten Borough.
        p.   cm. — (Maynooth studies in local history; No. 26)
    Includes bibliographical reference and index.
    ISBN 0–7165–2676–X (pbk.)
    1. Athlone (Ireland)—Politics and government. 2. Electioneering—Ireland—
Athlone—History—19th century. 3. Athlone (Ireland)—Social conditions.
I. Title.   II. Series.
    DA995.A75L46   1999
    320.9418'15'09034—dc21   99–31100
                                                              CIP

Typeset in 10 pt on 12 pt Bembo by
Carrigboy Typesetting Services, County Cork
Printed by ColourBooks Ltd, Dublin

Contents

Acknowledgements

I wish to express my gratitude to a number of people for their help in the completion of this work. Firstly, I wish to acknowledge my indebtedness to my father-in-law, the late Professor T.P. O'Neill, who introduced me to local history. My thanks to the Department of Modern History, Maynooth College, and in particular to Dr. Raymond Gillespie, whose course has been most enjoyable and stimulating. I am especially grateful to my supervisor, Dr. Mary Ann Lyons for her invaluable guidance and assistance. My thanks also to Gearóid O'Brien of Athlone Library who unselfishly shared his knowledge of Old Athlone. Finally, I would like to thank my wife Sinéad and my children, Fionnuala, Feidhlim, and Diarmuid for their patience and support.

Introduction

Until the introduction of the secret ballot in 1872 voting in parliamentary elections throughout Ireland and Britain was carried out in public. The names of electors and how they cast their votes were frequently published in the form of poll books or in local newspapers. In the context of small electorates that were often divided on religious or other factional lines, this meant that voters were subject to a variety of blandishments and menaces. That gave to nineteenth-century electoral contests a piquancy that no longer obtains and it also means that a study of elections and their allied activities at local level provides an intimate insight into the fabric of the community.

The purpose of this study is to examine the social structure of the parliamentary borough of Athlone in the period 1830–85 and, through an inquiry into the character of political activity, to illuminate the attitudes and social behaviour of its inhabitants. The history of electioneering in Athlone epitomises the corrupt political practices that were common throughout Ireland in the nineteenth century, and which earned for Athlone the sobriquet of 'the rotten borough'.[1] The year 1830 marked the first contested election in the borough since the Act of Union which had reduced the parliamentary representation of Athlone from two members to one, as had also occurred in the cases of thirty other boroughs.[2] The reforms of 1884–5 threw all but nine of the largest boroughs into new county constituencies, and in 1885 the borough of Athlone was closed and the town was incorporated in the constituencies of South Roscommon and South Westmeath.[3]

Political life has received comparatively little attention from local historians, who have tended to confine themselves to social and economic themes. K. Theodore Hoppen's standard work *Elections, politics and society in Ireland, 1832–1885* depicts local political communities in their wider context of social, economic, and cultural developments in society.[4] Borough politics is analysed by John B. O'Brien in 'Population, politics and society in Cork, 1780–1900', Ann Barry and Theodore Hoppen in 'Borough politics in O'Connellite Ireland: the Youghal poll books of 1835 and 1837', and Stephen A. Royle in 'The Lisburn by-elections of 1863'.[5] In addition R.V. Comerford's essay 'Tipperary representation at Westminster, 1801–1918' provides a survey of national electoral practice and the effect on it of the various reform measures throughout the nineteenth century, and includes an account of politics in the boroughs of Clonmel and Cashel.[6]

There is a sizeable body of historical writing on the town of Athlone but no detailed survey of the town in the nineteenth century has been attempted. The previous three centuries have been covered in a post graduate study by Harman Murtagh.[7] The introductory essay to *Irish Historic Towns Atlas: No. 6 Athlone* by the same author, traces the development of the town from earliest times to the present day, with an emphasis on the morphogenetic processes in the evolution of the townscape.[8] A number of essays concerned with specific nineteenth-century social and economic topics may be found in *Irish midland studies* edited by Harman Murtagh, *Athlone bridging the centuries* edited by Marian Keaney and Gearóid O'Brien, and the six numbers of the *Journal of the Old Athlone Society*.[9]

Newspapers provide the most continuous sequence of documentation in the body of available source material. The 'Moran manuscripts', a collection of newspaper cuttings relating to Athlone and surrounding districts served as an invaluable guide to significant local happenings and was therefore an indispensable starting point in undertaking this investigation.[10] A wide range of parliamentary papers has been consulted; those drawn on most extensively include census reports, election petitions and papers relating to education and local government. Griffith's Valuation (1854–55) has been used to examine the physical fabric and the social stratification of the town at mid century. Changes in the town's economic structure have been traced by an analysis of entries in trade directories. The records of the Chief Secretary's Office in the National Archives have provided valuable information on fenianism, while the Board of National Education records in the same repository, have yielded detailed information on all the local national schools. A polemical account of Irish politics written in 1886 by T.P. O'Connor, M.P. has been adverted to frequently for its exposition of borough politics in Athlone.

The first section of this study will set the scene by looking at Athlone through the eyes of contemporary observers, and using Griffith's Valuation to construct a profile of the town as it was in the middle of the nineteenth century. Changing aspects of the socio-economic and political life of the town will then be examined including an investigation of population trends, economic development, educational advances, and modernising trends in the functioning of local government. The second part deals with the emergence of a political community and focuses specifically on the local response to political developments in the O'Connellite era. Finally the political history of Athlone is traced from the first electoral victory of William Keogh in 1847 through to the closure of the borough in 1885.

Athlone and its changing social structure 1830–85

Situated near the geographical centre of Ireland, nineteenth-century Athlone was divided by the river Shannon into two almost equal parts. The west town lay in the barony of Athlone, in the county of Roscommon (until its transfer to Westmeath in 1899), and in the province of Connacht.[1] East Athlone was in the barony of Brawny, in County Westmeath in the province of Leinster. With the exception of a small portion in the parish of Kiltoom, the west town lay in the parish of St Peter, and the diocese of Elphin. The east side was part of the parish of St Mary, under the jurisdiction of the Catholic diocese of Ardagh and Clonmacnoise, and the Church of Ireland diocese of Meath. Athlone's location on the frontier of Leinster and Connacht placed it on the periphery of the adjoining civil and ecclesiastical administrative regions. The consequent failure to become either a cathedral or a county town had adverse effects on economic, social and intellectual development and was manifested in an impoverished architectural heritage.[2]

Visitors to Athlone in the nineteenth century were almost invariably disparaging of the town.[3] In 1832 Isaac Weld noted 'a total absence of symmetry . . . whether in reference to the style of the houses or the alignment of the streets, and a mixture of poor and indifferent houses with those of better description.'[4] The best private houses and the only street having any pretensions to cleanliness were situated in the Leinster division of the town.[5] On the Connacht side of the river he found 'cabins of the meanest description' inhabited by people 'whose appearance gave indication of the lowest state of civilisation'.[6] In 1834 H.D. Inglis declared 'Athlone is a remarkably ugly town. So deficient is it in good streets that after I had walked over the whole town, I still imagined I had seen only the suburbs'.[7] Another observer remarked 'you cannot walk in the streets of Athlone, you must wade. So inconceivably dirty a place does not exist in Europe'.[8] Half a century later, Athlone still 'seemed to be always muddy' with the result that on Sunday afternoon everyone went for a walk on the railway.[9] The narrow Elizabethan bridge was the cause of great congestion especially on market days when the scene of confusion presented was 'without parallel in Ireland.'[10] However, as part of a costly programme of improvements carried out under the auspices of the Shannon Commissioners, the old bridge was replaced by a wider structure that was completed in 1844.[11] This, together with the opening of a railway viaduct in 1851, and the provision of two fine sets of railway buildings by the competing Midland Great Western and Great Southern and Western companies, combined to alter substantially the street patterns and the riverine townscape.[12] In spite of such structural improvements, a traveller of 1852 wrote 'when we had seen its old castle, its two new and splendid bridges, its railway station and its barracks we had seen all'.[13]

The physical fabric of Athlone at mid century may be examined quantitatively using Griffith's Valuation, the most thorough inventory of property to date.[14] Out of a total number of 1,261 buildings, 68 per cent were below £5 valuation, and only 8 per cent were valued at more than £20. Although the description of tenements is limited, the absence of imposing buildings is evident. The most extensive urban landmark was the army barracks valued at £1,200 which occupied 32.5 acres in a prime central location on the riverfront and served as a major obstacle to development on the west bank. The only other buildings with a valuation of £50 or greater were the workhouse, at Abbey Lane; the Lock flour mills, Clonoun Road; an old distillery, Patrick Street; the castle, Castle Street, and the M.G.W. station house and associated refreshment rooms at Ranelagh. The more opulent residences and business premises were almost equally distributed on either side of the river, the main concentration being in Church Street, Northgate Street, Main Street, and Castle Street. Lodgers were almost exclusively segregated to the west side of town, where a ghetto of a sort had developed in the laneways in the vicinity of Connaught Street. One such street, Butler's Row, consisted of eighteen lots, fourteen of which were occupied by lodgers. The houses there were valued at £1 to £2, and as late as 1876 were found by a sanitary inspector to house pigs, to have piles of filth piled outside the front doors, and to be without privy accommodation due to the lack of back yards.[15]

As an indicator of status and prosperity the rateable valuation of a person's accommodation or property tells something of the social stratification of the urban community. In evidence before a parliamentary inquiry in 1876 the town clerk of Athlone, William Kelly, expressed the view that Athlone was different from other places in that while other towns had one proprietor of many houses, Athlone had many proprietors with a few properties each.[16] This, in his opinion, was the cause of the uncoordinated development and heterogeneous appearance of the town. There were indeed many lessors, 331 in all, of whom fifty-eight, or 18 per cent were women. At the head of the social pyramid, there was no one predominant proprietor capable of exercising a controlling influence. The Protestant educational charity, the Incorporated Society for the Promotion of Schools in Ireland, either alone, or in combination with others, held property to the value of £1,883. 11s. 0d. out of a total urban valuation of £10,426. 14s. 0d. This, and other absentee interests, has been blamed for the economic stagnation that affected Athlone in the eighteenth century.[17] Lord Castlemaine, who owned 8,854 statute acres with a valuation of £4,354, held a modest stake in the town itself, being the immediate lessor of forty-four properties with a cumulative valuation of £264.[18]

The impression that emerges from a study of the published valuations is one of a population that displayed few outward signs of prosperity. The vast majority of housing was of low valuation without the leavening effect of a resident gentry or professional class that might be associated with the institutions of a county town. The inhabitants of the town would have looked on an urban landscape that was uninspiring in architectural terms. The streets were the result of uncoordinated development and were flanked by housing of a very mean description. Fraser may have been harsh when stating that Athlone did not contain a single street fitted either for a general thoroughfare or business, but Griffith's Valuation of a decade later does little to disprove his contention.[19] The crude population statistics in Table 1, which are drawn from the census returns of 1831 to 1891, present a misleading impression of the demographic history of Athlone.[20]

The 1831 census measured the population of the borough of Athlone without specifying the extent of this unit. A contemporary report of commissioners appointed to delineate urban boundaries stated that the limits of the borough of Athlone, although not defined by any known boundary, were understood to include a circle with a radius of a mile and a half from the bridge over the Shannon.[21] This was the borough as prescribed by the governing charter with an area of 4,522 acres.[22] The same report proposed a boundary more closely congruent with the urban area with an extent of 485 acres, a total of 1,027 houses and a population of 6,161.[23] This geographical area accords closely with the town of 440 acres which was used as the basis of enumeration from 1841 to 1861, whereas the borough of 1831 encompassed a sizeable rural population. However, a further complication arises from the fact that the census commissioners of 1841 decided to omit the army serving in Ireland, together with their wives and families from the calculations.[24] Since an unknown number of these people were included in the earlier population estimates, the precise nature of the changes that occurred cannot be established, but it would appear that the urban area of Athlone experienced a population increase, from 6,161 in 1832, to 6,393 plus the military, in 1841.

Table 1 Extent, houses and population of Athlone, 1831–91

Year	1831	1841	1851	1861	1871	1881	1891
Total area in acres	4,522	440	440	440	1098	1129	1129
No. of inhabited houses	1,764	974	913	1006	1075	1104	1052
Population	11,406	6,393	6,214	5,902	6,565	6,755	6,742

Source: Census Reports 1831–91

The population of Athlone may in fact have risen by some 60 per cent from the beginning of the century till 1841. Window tax and hearth money tax returns have been used to calculate the total number of houses in Athlone in the period 1798 to 1800, at from 671 to 692, and from this a population level slightly in excess of 4,000 at the end of the eighteenth century has been posited.[25] This would give an annual growth rate of 1.15 per cent over a period of forty-one years. The expected growth rate in a pre-industrialised society is in the order of 0.5 per cent.[26] The effects of the Great Famine halted this upward spiral as the population total of 6,214 for 1851 demonstrates. Again the military were excluded in this figure as were the 1,766 inmates of the workhouse and four inmates in the Bridewell. The decline is continued in the following decade to reach 5,902, exclusive of 323 in the workhouse, two in the Bridewell and 825 in the military barracks in the townland of Ranelagh. The census returns of 1871, 1881, and 1891, for the township of Athlone, are inclusive of army personnel and their families, and workhouse inmates, officers and their families, which serves to disguise a further decline. The occupants of the workhouse numbered 325 in 1871, 310 in 1881, and 285 in 1891, while the military barracks contained 618 in 1871, 1,032 in 1881, and 1,026 in 1891. If these figures are discounted from the total, the remaining urban population amounts to 5,622 in 1871, 5,413 in 1881, and 5,431 in 1891. The latter figure represents a decline of 962, or 15.05 per cent, on the 1841 population. Furthermore, the urban area referred to as the township of Athlone was about two and a half times the size of the town referred to in the census reports from 1841 to 1861, thus the population decline in the built up area was even greater than these figures would indicate.

In 1861 and in each census that followed, the population of Athlone was divided by religious denominations. The figures for 1861 show that Roman Catholics accounted for 82 per cent of the urban population, Episcopalian Protestants 16 per cent, with Presbyterians and Methodists at just over 1 per cent. When the barracks was included in the urban total in 1871 the Roman Catholic share was reduced to 77 per cent. The religious balance was in fact the same as it had been a century and a half earlier. An estimate of the religious composition of eighteenth-century Athlone based on Bishop Synge's Religious census of 1749, put the Roman Catholic share of the population at about three quarters.[27] Athlone, in short, may be characterised as a garrison town, where Protestants constituted a sizeable proportion of the population. Overall the population of the town increased from 6,161 in 1832 to 6,742 in 1891. While the precise extent of population increase in the 1830s cannot be quantified for the reasons given above, the census reports show that the population declined at a rate of 0.41 per cent per annum between 1841 and 1881 and increased marginally in the next decade.

It was said of pre-Famine Athlone that, excepting its military importance, the town had turned its geographical centrality to surprisingly little practical account.[28] The town was not without manufacturing industry; there were in the 1830s two extensive distilleries, each providing from 40,000 to 50,000 gallons of whiskey annually, two tanneries, three soap and candle manu-factories, two breweries on a large scale, and several corn-mills.[29] However, employment levels in these industries cannot have been very high since only about fifty-five labourers were constantly employed in the two distilleries, brewery and tan yard that were located in St Peter's Parish.[30]

As a commercial centre Athlone fared better. Business in general was on the increase, in line with the rising population, and according to Isaac Weld in 1832, many additional shops had been opened.[31] This is borne out by an 88 per cent increase in the number of trade directory entries for Athlone between 1824 and 1846. There was no significant change over the following decades until 1881, when the number of entries was almost 20 per cent up on the figure for 1870. However, this increase which was also reflected in 1894 does not represent any real expansion in the town's trading functions, but rather the inclusion of a category not employed in previous directories, namely that of 'farmer in the town of Athlone'.

An examination of trade directories can be useful in tracing the fortunes of the master and employer sector of the labour force and in outlining the business structure of a town. In terms of the number of directory entries public houses and grocery outlets were predominant, but the evidence suggests that the entrepreneur or tradesman led a precarious existence, and in most cases the life span of the individual business was short. Twenty-four Athlone publicans were named in *Pigot's directory* of 1824, but not one of these remained in 1846; moreover only a single surname, that of McCann, survived on the facade of a public house, indicating that few businesses passed on from father to son.[32] It might be expected that there would be a high degree of continuity of surnames within certain trades as skills were passed on from father to son, but this does not appear to have been the case. Among the boot and shoemakers whose numbers were fairly stable, only one surname, that of Hopkins, is common to all directories from the 1820s to 1894.[33] The impression that trade and commerce provided an unstable financial base is underlined by a comparison of surnames in the directories of 1824 and 1894. Excluding nobility and clergy, there were 107 different surnames cited under Athlone in *Pigot's directory* of 1824, but only thirty of these names featured in Slater's more comprehensive *Directory* of 1894.[34]

The early census reports do not provide a detailed breakdown of the employment structure of Athlone, but the printed census returns for 1871, 1881, and 1891 show the numbers employed in some 200 different male occupations and almost half as many female occupations.[35] This information may be used to trace the fluctuations in the different occupational sectors as a whole.[36] The figures show that between 64 per cent and 70 per cent of Athlone's male population was engaged in gainful employment in these years, while among females the proportions thus employed was considerably less, being recorded at between 31 per cent and 46 per cent. Public service and professions, which included the military, accounted for the largest section of the working male population ranging from 37 per cent in 1871 to 42 per cent in 1891. Female employment was more heavily skewed in favour of one sector, namely domestic service, which declined from 65 per cent in 1871 to 47 per cent in 1891. An increase in male employment in manufacturing from 14 per cent in 1871 to 20 per cent in 1891 is accounted for by the expansion of two large employers, Athlone Woollen Mills in Northgate Street; and Shannon Sawmills in Distillery Lane. The high level of female employment in manufacturing, from 16 per cent in 1871 to 32 per cent in 1891, reflected the numbers of milliners and dressmakers and also the demand for female labour in the woollen mills. The wages in the mills were said to be on a somewhat higher scale than in the north of Ireland, but at the same time there was some complaint that a great number of the highest paid operatives were brought from Belfast.[37]

The growth of the woollen mills was the great success story of nineteenth-century Athlone, and in 1885 it was described as one of the most flourishing factories of woollens in the United Kingdom.[38] A factory was established by a Dr Gleeson in 1859 and had a lingering existence until 1869 when it was closed down.[39] In 1870 William Smith joined Dr Gleeson as a partner and revived the firm, but little progress was made for some five years except in training the workforce.[40] When the factory reopened it employed under fifty workers and the plant comprised ten looms, two sets of machines, and 650 spindles.[41] In 1885 employment had risen to nearly 350 hands with twelve sets of machines, 6,000 spindles, and sixty-six looms.[42] By then they were working the frieze for part of the Canadian Police winter uniforms and, according to the evidence of William Smith, had several times taken contracts for institutions 'in the middle of Scotch manufacturing districts'.[43]

It was symptomatic of the changing industrial structure that while the woollen mills was located on the site of a former brewery, Shannon Saw Mills, Athlone's other great industry of the post-Famine period, was developed on the site of a former distillery.[44] Established in 1860 the factory was employing up to 200 men in 1870, by which time it had become the largest converter of native timber in Ireland.[45] Wood used for upholstering work was manufactured and exported to the English market and to Scotland and America.[46]

In the early nineteenth century Athlone had two weekly markets, on Tuesdays and on Saturdays, and four annual fairs.[47] There was no market square and trading took place in the streets of the town.[48] The town commissioners eventually opened a fair green in 1856 by which time considerable numbers of cattle were moved by rail; in January of 1856 for example forty wagons of cattle were dispatched to Dublin in one day.[49] The number of fairs had risen to seven in 1889.[50] Nonetheless Athlone's fair never reached the stature of its nearby Moate counterpart since the land in its immediate vicinity was not fattening land, and as a centre for store cattle it was always dominated by Ballinasloe which was the main source of supply for the whole of the west midlands.[51]

A large corn market existed in the 1820s, vast quantities of grain being consumed by two extensive distilleries, a brewery, and by the mills of the town and neighbourhood.[52] In 1861 Athlone millers had an extensive inland trade sending immense quantities of flour to Clonmel, Rathkeale, Limerick and other places.[53] Slater's *Directory* of 1881 listed thirteen millers and corn merchants in and around Athlone. The main market was held in an open space under the wall supporting the castle mound and in addition to corn the articles of produce on sale included vegetables, potatoes, sheep, cattle, pigs, butter, eggs and fowl.[54] Great quantities of turf were brought to the town and sold. Fleets of little boats could be seen laden with turf in the canals, and elsewhere it was stacked in heaps larger than several three storey houses.[55] Large trout from the Shannon were sold for the 'merest trifle' and apparently were in less demand than eels, and saltwater fish were brought from Galway and sold in the Shambles, the site of the meat market.[56]

Overall Athlone was a multifunctional town drawing its economic strength from a variety of quarters. The town served as a centre for the marketing, processing, and distribution of agricultural produce. In 1803 an extensive scheme of defence works was commenced at 'The Batteries' west of Athlone and the town remained an important military centre throughout the nineteenth century.[57] Improved communications with the introduction of the steamboat in the 1830s and the railway in the 1850s at once contributed to the obsolescence of traditional manufacturing and attracted new industries such as the woollen mills.[58] The stagnation in trade and commerce after the Famine and the lack of continuity of employment in this sector would have placed many in straitened circumstances, a point of relevance to the discussion of politics which follows later.

The growth of an educated and literate public opinion in the nineteenth century was an important social development that had implications for the democratisation of Irish politics. The catalyst of educational change was the establishment of a system of national education by the Chief Secretary, Edward Stanley in 1831. The heterogeneous nature of the existing educational provision is documented in the second report of the Commissioners of Irish education inquiry that featured a countrywide educational census.[59] The structural changes consequent upon the growth of the new schools may be assessed by a comparison with a set of returns made in 1868.[60]

In 1824 Athlone had four free schools attended by an estimated 390 pupils, and seventeen pay schools with 611 pupils.[61] Many of the latter were little more than hedge schools. Evidently the master or mistress of the small hedge school was glad to accept a pupil of any denomination and likewise some parents were not deterred by the teacher's religion as almost all these schools were mixed. At one end of the spectrum was Launcelot Collins who taught thirty pupils in a smoky cabin in Brideswell for the meagre income of £8 per annum. In contrast was Richard O'Keeffe's school in Strand Street. The building was described as a large modern slated house and the master derived an income of £400 from thirty students. Each boarder had a separate bed, and the course of instruction included Latin grammar, Greek, French, the history of Rome, the history of England, geography and the use of the globe, mathematics, spelling, English grammar, writing and arithmetic.[62] Schools of this sort, often termed academies, commercial schools or classical schools, offered an intermediate or secondary type of education whereas the curriculum of the lowlier class of hedge school was essentially elementary in nature, providing basic literacy and arithmetical knowledge, and religious instruction.[63]

The ephemeral nature of the hedge school is shown by the fact that only four schools mentioned in the 1824 returns were still in existence in 1835.[64] A generation hence an even more radical restructuring had taken place.[65] All the hedge schools had disappeared to be replaced by only seven schools. This rationalisation was prompted by Stanley's institution of the Board of Commissioners of National Education in Ireland to oversee a state system of primary education. The response to educational reform was influenced by religion and political outlook. In 1835 Rev. Kieran Kilroe, parish priest of St Mary's, was instrumental in obtaining a site for the Anchors Bower school, but the Protestant rector Rev. James R. Moffatt 'peremptorily refused' to support his application for aid to the Board of Commissioners of National Education, due to his 'contempt of the whig government'.[66] The application was, however, endorsed by six Protestants, among whom was William Foster, grocer and wine merchant and member of the reform minded Independent Club of Athlone.[67] Rev. Martin O'Reilly of St Peter's parish also met with a lack of co-operation from the incumbent Rev. Hugh Murray in his foundation of the Deerpark school in 1844.[68] In 1857 Rev. O'Reilly backed the nuns of the Convent of Mercy in their efforts to establish St Peter's female school, saying it would confer the blessings of education on hundreds of poor children 'who otherwise would be strollers in the town of Athlone and its vicinity'; an apparent reference to the problem of prostitution endemic in the garrison town.[69] In contrast the Rev. Hugh Murray felt that the Deerpark school was 'quite adequate for the educational needs of the parish', and that a needless outlay of funds 'to promote conventual institutions', would 'only serve to increase the odium which some suppose the Board so justly deserves'.[70]

The 1868 returns reveal a shift to denominational schooling, with only seven pupils in the town attending a school which was not of their own persuasion. The Established Church opposed the National Board and set up their own school system under the Church Education Society which maintained St Peter's parochial school in Athlone. St Mary's parochial school was maintained by a private endowment supplemented with annual grants from the Board of Erasmus Smith.[71]

Although the national schools gave an opportunity for education into early adolescence or intermediate level, the majority of children stayed on for only two or three years.[72] Secondary education was generally a concern for the middle classes and its provision in Athlone or elsewhere was quite limited. In 1857 a diocesan college was established by the bishop of Elphin at Summerhill, a mile west of Athlone[73] but in 1880 the college was transferred to Sligo.[74] There was no replacement until the Marist Brothers established an intermediate school on the opposite side of the river in 1884.[75]

The Ranelagh Endowed School built in 1764, with the express purpose of educating poor Protestant boys, had by the mid-nineteenth century developed into a primary school with a secondary top.[76] Following the establishment of the Intermediate Education Board in 1878 enrolment grew steadily and in 1887 there was a total of 117 boys in the school, only two of whom were boarders.[77]

The long term impact of these structural changes in education is indicated by a comparison of the rate of illiteracy in 1841 and 1901. In 1841 33.9 per cent of the population of Athlone of five years and upwards could neither read nor write, while in 1901 the number had fallen to 12.3 per cent.[78] Much of the credit for this improvement must be ascribed to the initiative of Edward Stanley and those who implemented it at a local level. Of particular significance was the leading role played by the parish priests Frs Kilroe and O'Reilly in the establishment of the national schools. This was part of a wider involvement in public life which saw both men figure prominently in the political life of the borough. The contrast in the response of the churches to educational reform also serves as a useful pointer to the lines of political division in the community.

'To the prosperity of Athlone the corporation have at no time contributed, nor is it likely that, as present constituted, they ever will'.[79] This unequivocal censure from the commissioners on the state of municipal corporations in Ireland, was to be the epitaph of a municipal body which derived its authority from a charter of James I in 1606. Exasperation with this and other similarly retrograde corporations led to their abolition by an act of 1840 under which Athlone town commissioners came into existence.[80] The officers of the corporation comprised a sovereign, two bailiffs, thirteen burgesses including the constable of the castle, a recorder, a town clerk, a sergeant at arms and a billet master.[81] There was also a select and secretive body called the common council in which the management of the affairs of the borough was nominally vested.[82] In reality the entire control of the corporation was exercised by the first Baron Castlemaine, William Handcock. The council had the power of self election in that its members were elected for life by the common council itself, from the ranks of the burgesses and freeholders who themselves had been elected by the common council. This enabled 'the patron', however large the number of freemen might be, to maintain a very close and exclusive corporation. Those elected were said to be either the nominees of his Lordship, or persons notoriously in his interest. No Roman Catholic had ever been a member of the council, or a burgess.

William Handcock had become the first Baron Castlemaine of Moydrum in 1812, when he was rewarded for accommodating the government of the day with his parliamentary seat of Athlone.[83] The viscounty of Castlemaine followed in 1822.[84] The Handcock residence at Moydrum Castle, about a mile and a half from Athlone was a solid castellated mansion with square turrets at each angle, beautifully situated on the edge of a small lake, and surrounded by an extensive and richly wooded demesne.[85] The progenitor of this, the largest landed family in the Athlone area, was another William Handcock, who had acquired about 1,000 acres in the barony of Brawny in the Cromwellian settlement, which he augmented to 5,000 acres by 1680.[86] Thereafter various Handcocks served as M.P. for Athlone, and by the time of the Union the borough appears to have been effectively controlled by two families, the Handcocks and the St Georges.[87] The Act of Union disfranchised eighty-four Irish boroughs and converted thirty-one of the thirty-three retained boroughs, including Athlone, into single-member constituencies.[88] Subsequently Richard St George who had opposed the measure sold his interest in the Athlone seat to the Handcocks and resigned from parliament.[89] William Handcock served as M.P. for Athlone until 1803 and exercised political control of the borough until the 1830s.[90]

The functioning of the corporation throughout the nineteenth century was characterised by inaction, dereliction and misconduct. The inhabitants of the town complained that the revenues of the corporation were applied, contrary to the express provisions of the charter, to the payment of municipal officers who rendered no service to the community.[91] The receipts from September 1831 to 1832 showed that £220 was obtained for the rent of customs and cranage (charges for the use of the weighing crane), of which only £50 was spent on street repairs. The following year nothing whatever was spent on the cleaning and repair of the streets or on the bridge which was in an exceedingly dangerous state. The sovereign as clerk of the market occasionally attended to its regulation but this duty was by no means diligently performed and he rarely inquired after fraudulent weights and measures.[92]

The administration of justice also contributed to popular resentment. There was no police, save the sergeant at mace and four members of the county constabulary, who were stationed in the town. There was no night watch. Town constables had been appointed from 1816 to 1826.[93] It was stated that these men were principally requited for their services by the seizure of cattle found on the public ways within the borough, for the purpose of fining the owners and obtaining a moiety of the penalty. It was not unknown for the constable to drive cattle from their enclosures onto the roads in order to subject their owners to fines, or to extort money from them.[94] Another dubious practice related to the civil court of the borough which notwithstanding the discontinuance of its sitting in the early 1820s, continued to effect seizures under its processes. Upon an unsworn verbal statement an attachment could be issued against the goods of any persons within the bounds of the borough. When bail could not be procured as might happen in the case of strangers especially, the defendant was coerced to settle no matter how unjust the claims as the only means of getting back his goods. The effect of these circumstances was a distrust in the administration of justice and a spirit of resistance to constituted authority.[95]

The replacement of this self-perpetuating clique by town commissioners in 1840 was followed by modest infrastructural improvements, under the constraints of limited powers of town management and a reluctance on the part of the commissioners to over-burden the rate payers who elected them. The composition of the new body presented a pointed contrast to the old corporation. The first commissioners included a Catholic priest, Rev. Kieran Kilroe P.P. of St Mary's.[96] Rev. Martin O'Reilly P.P. of St Peter's who topped the poll with 205 votes, and Rev. J.J. O'Donovan of the Franciscan Friary, joined Rev. Kilroe following their successes in the 1843 election, and in 1851 Rev. O'Reilly was unanimously elected chairman.[97] Initially town commissioners in Ireland were chosen by the electors, the £5 householders, from amongst residents rated at £20 or more.[98] Under an act of 1854 the electorate was expanded to include all those households at £4 or above, together with lessors of property valued at £50 or over, and the commissioners were to be rate payers valued at £12 or over.[99] Not until 1880 did all voters become eligible for membership of town bodies.[100] This ensured that the commissioners were drawn from a relatively small pool of the well to do. In 1876 for example, those entitled to vote as owners, occupiers, or lessors numbered 365, while potential representatives, with valuation of £12 and upwards, amounted to 127.[101]

The parsimony of the ratepayers was not the least of the difficulties that the town commissioners had to contend with. In 1850 a meeting of the inhabitants of Athlone was held at the courthouse for the purpose of considering the propriety of extending the powers of the town commissioners to lighting and watching.[102] As draper and town commissioner Mr John McDonnell spoke in favour of the proposal the body of the courthouse was in uproar.[103] Amidst yelling and shouting nothing could be heard but 'overtaxed', 'want no light', 'humbug', 'scheme job'. The proposal was rejected on a show of hands, but upon scrutiny and the exclusion of ineligible voters, the result was sixty-five votes in favour and forty-six against. A gasworks was eventually constructed at Northgate Street and street lighting was introduced in 1855.[104]

Less progress was made in dealing with the condition of the streets. The special act of parliament required to transfer control of the roads, footpaths, bridges and public works in the borough, from the Grand Juries of Roscommon and Westmeath, was not forthcoming until 1894.[105] A newspaper in 1887 complained that the condition of the streets was a scandal and that it would require a cart whip to get those employed on the streets to do the work properly.[106] High Street and Queen Street were identified as the worst and most neglected streets, and the importation of Chinese labour was facetiously suggested by the writer, as they were famous for their diligence.[107]

A more pressing concern was the threat to public health posed by the poor sanitary condition of the town. The prevalence of typhus fever in 1869 was attributed to the effluence from surface drains, and the town commissioners were said to have been withheld from taking action by the consideration of the expense that would be involved.[108] There was no connected system of covered sewers, and the few that did exist were found in the immediate vicinity of the military barracks and the lower parts of the town. In the upper parts of the town on both sides, liquid sewage for the most part flowed by surface drains from one back yard to another, accumulating as it issued into the street, frequently under or through an inhabited house, and continued its course by the margin of the footpath to the lower end of the town. Here it was either discharged into a covered sewer, or, collecting into a fetid pool, it was ultimately absorbed into the soil, or diffused by evaporation into the atmosphere.[109] Under the Public Health Act of 1874 the town commissioners were created the urban sanitary authority with the power to set an unlimited rate for sanitary purposes, but it was not until 1895 that a waterworks and sewerage scheme was completed in Athlone.[110] In this instance too, an element of the ratepayers had opposed the scheme on the grounds of expense.[111]

It is worth pointing out that Athlone compares favourably in terms of expenditure with other towns such as Ennis, Kinsale, or Dungarvan.[112] Twenty-nine municipal towns exceeded Athlone in terms of population in the year 1866, but only twelve surpassed it in expenditure, while in 1876 fifteen towns spent more than Athlone.[113] In the context of the division of responsibilities with the Grand Juries, limited financial resources, and increasing obligations, the Athlone town commissioners acquitted themselves relatively well, both in comparison with their predecessors, and in national terms.

This section has looked at changes in society. Government intervention is seen to have created new structures in the areas of local government and education, while changes in the economy may be linked to demographic developments and improvements in communications. The next part of this study will focus on political life in the borough.

The political community in the era of O'Connell

The Act of Union preserved Athlone as a parliamentary borough with the right to return one member to the United Kingdom parliament. In 1832 a report to the Chief Secretary of Ireland declared that the electorate had always been under some particular influence, in consequence of which the borough was one of the closest in the kingdom.[1] Athlone was generally represented by a tory Handcock and a whig St George in the eighteenth-century Irish parliaments and there is only occasional record of contested elections despite the fact that neither family had dominant property interests in the town.[2] After the Union the dominion of the Handcock family over the one remaining parliamentary seat went unchallenged until the general election of 1830 when James Talbot stood unsuccessfully against Richard Handcock as a whig, or anti-corporation, candidate.[3] It was common to find candidates returned without opposition in the early nineteenth century. Nine boroughs had their first electoral contest since the Union in 1832, namely, Armagh, Belfast, Carlow, Clonmel, Dundalk, Ennis, Portarlington, Sligo, and Tralee.[4] Others had to wait even longer, Lisburn dominated by the local tory landlord Lord Hertford, witnessed its first contest of the century in 1852, when the Liberal, Roger Smyth, was victorious.[5] The emergence of an opposition to the former political monopoly of the Handcocks may be said to mark the beginnings of an active political community in Athlone, which owed its existence to a conjunction of local and national forces. Discontent over tolls and customs and the general behaviour of the corporation was the animating force behind a protest movement which arose in the 1820s. At the same time, the wider struggle for Catholic Emancipation was effecting a transformation in the political consciousness of the Irish people which led to the emergence of political activists at local level.[6]

Prior to the Irish Reform Act of 1832, Athlone was but one of twenty corporate boroughs that were under the control of a local landlord.[7] These included Cashel, whose leading interest was Richard Pennefather, Clonmel controlled by John, and after 1806 William Bagwell, Coleraine under Lord Waterford and Dundalk under Lord Roden.[8] As was the case in Cashel and Dundalk, the Athlone seat was usually sold to an outsider.[9] In 1831 these twenty boroughs had a total population of 212,935, but the franchise was restricted to only 1,925 men who were either members of the governing bodies or freemen.[10] The electorate in that year varied in size from 591 in Wexford, 451 in Londonderry, and 261 in Youghal, to twelve in Dungannon, thirteen in Sligo and twenty-six in Cashel. In Athlone the right to vote was confined to seventy-one freemen voters in 1831, of whom thirty-three were resident in the borough. The composition of the electorate was related to the preservation and advancement of factional interests. An attempt was made to broaden the constituency in 1829 when 350 residents 'comprising most of the respectable inhabitants' applied to be admitted free and tendered £1 each, with their petition to the sovereign. However, being supposed to be hostile to the Handcock family, they were all refused permission.[11] On 24 June 1831, 165 new freemen, including nine Catholics were admitted for the purpose of increasing the constituency in the interests of Lord Castlemaine's family, but that design was frustrated by the Reform Act of 1832 which declared that honorary freemen admitted subsequently to 30 March 1831 were not entitled to vote at elections for members of parliament.[12] The Reform Act confined the franchise to existing freemen who resided within seven miles of the town, whereas before 1832 the geographical location of voters had been irrelevant.[13] However, the electorate was expanded by the inclusion of those who occupied houses worth at least £10 a year.[14] This increased the electorate of Athlone to 243 for the general election of 1832 and, for the first time, gave Catholics who constituted over three quarters of Athlone's population, a say in parliamentary politics.[15]

One of the first important episodes in the development of local political consciousness centred on the eruption of popular discontent in 1826 regarding the corporation's administration of tolls and customs. This was part of a wider national campaign inspired by Thomas Spring Rice, M.P. for Limerick City, to press for the reduction or abolition of tolls.[16] Corn growers and small farmers in the vicinity of Athlone preferred to send their corn to neighbouring towns at a loss rather than submit to the exactions at the toll gates of Athlone.[17] Business interests in the town became concerned at the effects of such arbitrary confiscations on trade. A meeting of the inhabitants of the town and neighbourhood was held on 23 May 1826 at which Mr John Boswell of Boswell's Brewery in Northgate Street, and a barrister by profession, presided.[18] Boswell, 'a liberal Protestant' who later contributed to the Catholic rent, declared that although not a member of the corporation he wished to mediate between the conflicting parties in order to reach a settlement.[19] Another Protestant, Mr Christopher Robinson, a distiller, said that he could vouch for the fact that the town was being injured by corn being drafted to Birr by persons near the town.[20] Arthur Robinson, Christopher's brother and partner, expressed the view that the borough constables' conduct was even more galling than the exactions they practised, and proposed to give the most determined opposition to the tolls and customs.[21] When the adjourned meeting was resumed, it was resolved to investigate the commercial rights and privileges of the inhabitants of Athlone and vicinity, and also to demand the restoration of the amenities of the said town.[22]

The Corporation duly relented in the face of this pressure, and on 16 October 1826 Richard Handcock, senior vice-sovereign of Athlone, entered into an agreement on the part of the corporation in order to restore peace and good order.[23] The sum to be exacted in tolls was to be reduced from £400 to £200, but the abatement did not succeed in quelling discontent, and at the January fair of 1827 the people who collected the tolls received a severe beating, one man having three of his teeth knocked out.[24]

Local opposition was not sufficiently organised to thwart the customary return of Lord Castlemaine's nominee, Richard Handcock, in the 1826 general election, but while Castlemaine's position remained secure, the county constituencies experienced a major revolt of Catholic freeholders against landlord control, and in favour of Catholic Emancipation.[25] The victory of Tuite in Westmeath was one of the more notable triumphs and, in Roscommon, Catholic interests united to return Arthur French without a contest.[26] The success of the Catholic Association led to the steady development of local political organisations, and in 1827 the Liberal or Independent Club of County Louth became a model for clubs established in County Roscommon and elsewhere.[27] In 1828 seventy members of the Roscommon Liberal Club dined together at the assizes and planned to meet again at Boyle, Athlone, Strokestown and Castlerea.[28] About this time too, the Friends of Civil and Religious Liberty held meetings in Roscommon town, Ballinasloe and Mullingar.[29] In Athlone a Liberal club consisting of local residents petitioned parliament on four occasions between 1829 and 1830 in favour of the vote being vested solely in resident freemen.[30] At a public dinner at Dowd's Hotel in Athlone in 1830, speakers attacked the 'Corporation oppression which the people labour under'.[31] The meeting was presided over by Mr Christopher Dillon, a Protestant, who had spoken at the earlier meeting on tolls, and Peter Norton, a Catholic woollen draper of Church Street, presented a spirited exposé on the corporation.[32] The speakers also included the Reverends Browne, Kilroe, O'Reilly and McLoughlin, presaging the increasingly active role of the Catholic clergy in political affairs.

The response of the corporation to the rising tide of opposition demonstrates how non-electors, even those from outside the borough, played a part in the political process. On 24 June 1830 the corporation of Athlone held their common council.[33] At an early hour hundreds of the 'peasantry' were flocking into the town.[34] On being questioned as to what brought so many of them into Athlone some responded that they were the tenants of Lord Castlemaine.[35] Others said that their landlord the M.P. for Athlone Mr Richard Handcock, had ordered them into Athlone to marshall in his favour. When Lord Castlemaine left the meeting he was followed by hundreds cheering him, and Richard Handcock was 'chaired' through the town. When they came to the houses of Mr Norton and Mr Dillon the mob halted in derision, and upon crossing the bridge to the Connacht side, they commenced an assault on the houses of Messrs Fleming and Holton, 'liberal Protestants' who had joined the anti corporation party. Volleys of stones were thrown in the ensuing hostilities and the M.P. was forced to flee across the Shannon by boat. The following day a large counter demonstration, chaired by George Fleming, passed a resolution condemning the attempt made to silence public opinion by brute force and resolving 'that public liberty has been assailed and law and order violated, and the authors and encouragers of such violation are unfit to be the preservers of public peace or the depositories of the suffrages of the people'.[36] Coincident with this meeting an address from the Liberal Club, of which Daniel O'Connell was president, was posted all over the town.[37] The notice urged the inhabitants of Athlone to labour for a fair representation by extending the number of constituents. The anti corporation party proceeded to invite James Talbot, eldest son of the third baron Talbot de Malahide, to stand as a Liberal on their behalf in the forthcoming election.[38] Popular support, however, proved no substitute for a representative electorate, and Handcock was returned with thirty-seven votes to two for Talbot.[39]

The inchoate political organisation survived this wholly expected defeat and the following year Talbot, when invited to attend a dinner hosted by the Independent Club of Athlone, was met by a crowd of nearly 20,000.[40] The Independent Club was comprised of a cross section of the prosperous urban middle class.[41] The Protestant members included: the chairman Christopher Dillon, one time distiller and owner of boats that conveyed goods to Dublin; William Foster, grocer, wine merchant, publican and ironmonger; Robert Mercer Jameson, farmer; and George Fleming, leather seller, provision dealer and tallow chandler.[42] The Catholic clergy was represented by Reverends Kieran Kilroe, Martin O'Reilly and George J.P. Browne, later bishop of Galway and of Elphin. Among the prominent Catholic laymen were: William H. O'Connell, physician and surgeon; Peter Norton, woollen draper; Denis Kelly, apothecary; and Fergus Moriarty, haberdasher.[43] Once again the electorate proved unresponsive, and Handcock was returned, by a margin of thirty-three votes to two, in the election held on 4 May 1831.[44] On the next occasion, however, the *Freeman's Journal* could confidently proclaim a week before the election that the Castlemaine autocracy was annihilated in the Athlone borough, that the Reform Bill had made the people a power, and that they were resolved to exercise it for the public good.[45] On this occasion, with an electorate expanded to include £10 householders, Talbot was indeed victorious, securing 125 votes to 104 for Handcock, the first time since the Union that Castlemaine's electoral wishes had been frustrated.[46]

Talbot's performance in parliament proved a disappointment to his followers. His first act in the House was to vote for the tory nominee for Speaker, and his failure to support O'Connell in a division on the Coercion Bill was publicly condemned by the Athlone Trades Political Union, who resolved to displace him if he did not reverse his conduct.[47] At the run up to the next election in 1835 some cracks appeared in the liberal alliance. Rev. O'Reilly P.P. of St Peter's parish, and Rev. Kilroe P.P. of St Mary's parish wished their candidate to be bound by pledges to obey the will of the local organisation while distiller, John O'Beirne, felt that the majority should be guided by 'the wealthy, the influential and independent portion of the liberal and intelligent electors'.[48] Sectarian passions were inflamed by events in the tithe war, and at a meeting of electors in the yard adjoining St Peter's chapel on 26 December 1834 Rev. O'Reilly spoke of the 'crimsoned' fields of Rathcormac and suggested that an 'honest young Catholic' might stand for the borough.[49] In the event Talbot received the nomination, but lost the election, with eighty-three votes to ninety-six for Captain George B. Mathew, the tory candidate nominated by the Handcock family.[50] The outcome caused little disappointment to the reformers; the *Freeman's Journal* characterised the result as the replacement of a nominal reformer by an avowed tory, and professed not to regret the outcome.[51] Nationally the Conservatives managed to win thirty-seven of the 105 Irish seats, but this Athlone election, like many that followed, is of interest less for the result, or even the issues discussed, than for the conduct of the election and the light it throws on local society and political behaviour.[52]

The meagre increase in the electorate was sufficient to upset the long-established patronage of the borough, but in its place a new system took root. In a retrospect on the borough in the *Freeman's Journal* in 1885, Captain Mathew was credited with introducing to the electoral contest the bribery that earned for Athlone the sobriquet of "The Rotten Borough'.[53] Talbot was certainly quick to express his deep indignation against those who had first promised him support and then deserted him.[54] According to the local Liberal newspaper, *The Athlone Sentinel*, Mathew discovered soon after his arrival in Athlone that the Handcock influence might not be enough to secure his return and he promptly set to work to bribe, to corrupt, and to intimidate the independent electors.[55] That Catholics would vote for the tory candidate was considered an act of treachery, and the *Sentinel* in pursuance of its duty, published the names, addresses, and occupations of twenty-nine 'base and recreant Roman Catholics who had the audacious effrontery to come before the virtuous gaze of their brother electors and register their votes against the country'.[56] Also identified for public opprobrium were the fourteen voters who 'ran away at the instance of Mathew rather than vote honestly and fairly', and four other electors who declined to vote.

Were these electors who braved the obloquy of their co-religionists possessed of any distinguishing characteristics that might account for their actions? Spatial ties of parish or neighbourhood do not appear to have been determinants of electoral behaviour as twenty-three of the forty-seven voters or abstainers came from the Roscommon side of town, while the Handcock seat was in County Westmeath. Nor was there any occupational affinity among the Catholic tories. Publicans, shopkeepers, and butchers accounted for just less than half of the total, but tradesmen were also well represented with saddlers, shoemakers, gunsmiths, a mason, and a tailor being among their number. Also included in the miscellany were farmers, labourers, lodging house keepers, a medical doctor and a school teacher. Indigence may have left some electors susceptible to bribery. Owen Murphy of Irishtown was described as a 'struggling butcher' while Edward Henry, a publican from High Street had a net annual valuation in the Athlone Union rate book of only £5.[57] However, the same source shows the average valuation of eighteen of these electors to be a healthy £17 which implies that the process of persuasion may have been expensive. The case of Luke Tully, a publican and shopkeeper of Connaught Street provides an illustration. Just a few days previous to the election Tully was a member of a committee established to support Talbot.[58] However, the day before the election Tully's public house was selected as an open house for the reception of Mathew's friends. The practice of 'treating' as it was called, was a common feature of both Irish and English elections at this time, serving the dual purpose of enriching the publican and ingratiating the candidate with the populace. At Clonmel in 1835 the electorate was inveigled by free drink, free food and free dancing with 'immoral women'.[59] Tully is likely to have benefited from an extravagant hiring fee for his establishment as well as the large orders for drink; in any event the erstwhile 'noisy brawling patriot', hired a car and drove off to Dublin as soon as the election started, and thus avoided the necessity of voting for Talbot.[60]

Following the return of Mathew the electors led by Rev. O'Reilly and Rev. Kilroe made early plans to secure the election of John O'Connell, third son of Daniel O'Connell, at the next opportunity.[61] Two register inspectors sent to Athlone by the General Association found an active and efficient political organisation on the ground under the name of the Athlone Political Union.[62] This was now the only political society existing in the borough and its twin objects were the extension of the liberal franchise and the collection of the Justice Rents 'for the protection of the honest electors and other legal purposes'.[63] The registration of voters was attended to with great seriousness and was the subject of much disputation. At six a.m. on 5 April 1837 nine cars were drawn up in Athlone, on which were seated twenty-nine claimants of the franchise.[64] They proceeded to Moate sessions accompanied by Rev. Martin O'Reilly and others. In one case Mr Abbott Peacock was put up by the Conservatives to dispute the valuation of the property of a Mr Dillon, but upon examination Mr Peacock admitted that he was never in the house and could not tell its dimensions. However, despite the evidence of an architect who had surveyed the house and pronounced it worth £10 a year, the claim was rejected. In the evening the cortège with its twenty-two successful claimants returned to Athlone bedecked with laurel branches. Liberal success at the registries, Daniel O'Connell's slogan 'Justice for Ireland' which implied confidence in Melbourne's administration, and a strong candidate in John

O'Connell apparently convinced the conservatives that the cause was futile, and the young O'Connell was returned without a contest in the 1837 general election.[65] The election of a Catholic repealer encapsulates the magnitude of political change when compared with the return of Richard Handcock just over a decade previously. However, Daniel O'Connell himself acknowledged that the constituency of the borough of Athlone was very small and registered eighty 'orange' voters, thus twenty-five voters would have been sufficient to tip the scales the other way.[66]

John O'Connell's decision to transfer to Kilkenny City in the 1841 general election led to a contest for the Liberal nomination in Athlone between Edmund O'Beirne, a Dublin solicitor, and Daniel H. Farrell of Beechwood, County Roscommon.[67] O'Beirne had acted on behalf of the inhabitants of Athlone in their action against the corporation during the tolls controversy in 1826, and he enjoyed the recommendation of the Rev. O'Reilly; nonetheless Farrell was the chosen candidate. Under questioning from Rev. Kilroe in January 1841, Farrell revealed that he had not yet seriously entertained the idea of Repeal, and was unwilling to pledge himself to it, but this satisfied the majority of the Liberal electors who were more anxious to select a 'thorough supporter of the present government', than to become embroiled in the 'agitation of any abstract questions, whatever'.[68] The choice of George de la Poer Beresford, a connection of the Marquis of Waterford, as the Conservative candidate had the effect of polarising the contest on religious lines. Rev. O'Reilly warned that 'the priest hunting Beresford is come to town with the pitch cap and triangle', and implored voters in the name of suffering humanity 'to be one man in this glorious struggle'.[69] Erstwhile 'liberal Protestants' George Fleming and William Holton who had been leading members of the anti corporation party voted for the Conservative candidate.[70] In the words of the *Athlone Mirror*, 'every Protestant, both of the town and surrounding country, from the shop boy and the menial of the Incorporated Society, up to the nobleman, has clubbed together and made common cause against the nascent liberties of a newly enfranchised people'.[71] According to this analysis a 'few malcontent Protestants' had, out of disaffection or resentment, dallied with the popular party, but the moment that this struggle was over, and when they 'saw the inhabitants were about availing themselves of the privileges of subjects as granted them by the Reform Act', they instantly fled back to their own ground. The *Mirror* concluded that the reformers of the town were now confined to the Catholics alone and that they should throw overboard all Protestant fellowship and depend entirely upon themselves.

The bizarre conduct of the election undoubtedly contributed to this sense of grievance. On the first day of polling, Farrell's supporters, amounting to 114, assembled in Connaught Street 'each having a rose in his bosom', and marshalling themselves into lines of three men deep, marched to the hustings.[72] There, to the astonishment of all concerned, the assessor proceeded to reject the first six freeholders presented on the Liberal side, on the grounds that the description of tenure was not properly filled in, in the voting certificate.[73] The greater part of Farrell's supporters were rejected in similar manner, leaving Beresford the victor by thirty votes to seventeen.[74] The inevitable petition to parliament resulted in the unseating of Beresford with the poll amended to 110 for Farrell and sixty for Beresford.[75] Significantly, those who voted for Farrell included a number of men who had previously been accused of accepting bribes from Captain Mathew the Conservative victor in the 1835 election, men such as Gamuel Jervis and James Roper.[76] The political change of heart at this stage might not be unrelated to the eventual unseating of Farrell himself on the grounds of his having 'treated' the electors at Mr John Dowd's public house, 'The Three Blacks'.[77] Thus the evidence suggests that while rising sectarian tensions may have led Protestants to desert the Liberal camp, some of the Catholic converts to Farrell's side may have had motives that were more pragmatic than ideological.

The 1843 by-election was a significant episode which exposed the intensity of intimidation and the prevalence of bribery in Athlone politics in this period. It also confirmed that Athlone's Protestants had disavowed liberal politics and provided further evidence of the existence of a cohort of mercenary Catholic voters. The disqualified Farrell introduced John Collett, the son of an English merchant, to stand in his stead. Collett proclaimed his principles to be 'the firm and continued advocacy of civil and religious liberty', and somewhat implausibly suggested that as a free and independent Englishman residing in the neighbourhood of the House of Commons he would be better able to attend to the interests of Athlone.[78] His opponent, George de la Poer Beresford, was equally non-committal with regard to his programme, beyond stating that he supported the then Conservative government.[79]

The election commenced on Friday 31 March and ended on Tuesday 4 April in the return of Mr Collett by 114 votes to 108.[80] The *Athlone Sentinel* published the names of those who voted for each candidate and revealed that not a single Protestant had voted for Collett.[81] On this occasion, the thirteen Catholic voters who supported Beresford were conveniently identified by means of a cross beside the individual's name, which again highlights the pressures to which voters were subject in the era prior to the introduction of the ballot in 1872. After a quiet start to the polling the good humour of the occasion was shattered on the Saturday when Broderick and Larkin, two Catholic voters, were arrested by Beresford supporters under civil bill decrees for debt, while going from the tally room to the poll.[82] Broderick escaped into the booth and voted (for Collett), after which he was arrested and sent to jail. Larkin was dragged by the Beresford mob, flourishing sticks and screaming, into a place forming part of the tally room and was detained by force.[83] The petty sessions clerk, Mr Peacock, was identified as having held the man until the bailiff came up and laid hold of him. Eventually after much argument and threats of legal action, the debt was remitted and Larkin was allowed to cast his vote.[84]

On Sunday 2 April 1843 there was great excitement throughout the entire day as a report circulated that some of the poorer Catholic voters, as yet unpolled, would leave town during the night and thus their votes would be lost to the Liberal side. The relative strength of the parties being so equal this loss could have proved decisive and consequently a great number of Mr Collett's agents paraded the town in parties of between six and twelve throughout the entire night in order to prevent the voters from absconding. Beresford's agents were also on the watch but fortuitously no collision took place between them. On the Monday, one of the Catholic voters named Thomas Regan who had gone away on the first night of the election, came back to town, and it was believed that he was going to vote for Beresford.[85] When the news spread through the crowd the greatest excitement prevailed. Regan's daughter was brought into the polling booth and placed beside the professional men engaged on the Liberal side. Shortly after, a carriage guarded by the Lancers drove into the yard, and in a few minutes Regan, accompanied by Mr Osbourne, nephew to the Viscount Castlemaine, and a 'posse of street agents', made his appearance in the booth. Immediately a murmur ran through the crowd who sent up cries of 'take care you don't perjure yourself'. The daughter cried out 'father don't disgrace us all, or damn your soul', upon which Beresford's men insisted the girl should be removed and the booth cleared. Regan then proceeded to vote for Beresford. John Dowd (onetime supporter of the Liberal candidate Farrell), then drove up in a close carriage to a chorus of yells and execrations. Some of his friends rushed through the crowd to endeavour to secure him and prevent him from voting, but they were driven back by Beresford and his followers and Dowd too cast his vote for Beresford.

On Tuesday events took a Gilbertian turn when a carriage containing three persons disguised in large cloaks and moustaches drove into town. The carriage was occupied by two Westmeath magistrates, St George Gray and Edward Hudson, and Michael Lennon 'the horse breaker', the latter being one of the Catholic voters who had absconded. St George Grey came into the booth leading a person muffled in a large white outside coat 'a world too wide for him'. The collar of the coat was turned up, covering his ears and meeting above his eyebrows, and a cap was drawn down on his forehead, the peak of which carefully concealed his face. Lennon's wife who had been placed in the booth some time before cried out 'Micky a vick [sic], don't perjure yourself and disgrace your family', and she was ordered out of the booth by the police. Lennon took the oath in a scarcely audible voice, and still leaning on the arm of Mr Gray declared that he wished to vote 'for the good of the country and town, and for Captain Beresford'.

There was further commotion on Tuesday evening when the day coach which was expected to bring some more voters failed to arrive on time. The friends of one of these voters had gone on the night before towards Kinnegad and it was expected that they would try to stop him by force. A troop of police and military were sent to protect the voters and a party of Lancers were drawn up in front of a group of 500 people at Haire's Hotel in Athlone. A violent outcome seemed a possibility. When the coach arrived there was only one voter on board, Michael Lennon, a tailor from Castle Street. In this case, it was the voter's father who vainly besought him 'not to bring dishonour on his grey hairs, but to vote for his God and his country'. Rev. Martin O'Reilly then came forward and denounced perjury and corruption and said that as a Christian minister he could not but grieve over the infamy some renegade Catholics had brought on themselves and their religion, but above all on the injury they had inflicted on their immortal souls.

The drama that unfolded in the course of these five days involved the orchestration of a range of *dramatis personae* extending far beyond the small electorate. The extraneous candidates and their supporters, the friends and relatives of the electors, the police, the army, the election officials, and not least, the 'mob' all constituted an intimidating live audience before which the voter had to make his declaration. Women too, who were without the franchise, found an outlet for their political feelings at the hustings. Catholic voters were subject to the wrath of their priests and all were liable to vilification in the press. Despite the active participation of all these non-electors, the 1843 by-election was considered by the *Sentinel* to have been conducted with great propriety, 'there was no spitting, no throwing of filth or gutter of any description', and this happy state of affairs was chiefly attributable to the people 'taking the advice of the Roman Catholic clergy and that of the leaders of the popular party, who never ceased inculcating peace and good order'.[86] The gratified tone of this piece suggests that the absence of electoral violence was worthy of explanation, and indeed violence had become an increasingly common feature of elections nationally, after the mobilisation achieved by O'Connell, and the franchise changes of 1832.[87] In 1841, for example, a Cork candidate wrote how 'one of my voters after giving his vote was murdered, another lies at the point of death from a compound fracture of the skull; many have been cruelly beaten, their houses fired, others destroyed and the furniture burned before the doors'.[88] But while voting, or even abstaining, could have deleterious consequences, the burden of the franchise also had its compensations.

Collett departed from Athlone leaving strong proofs of his munificence in the shape of donations of £50 each to St Peter's chapel, Longford Cathedral, and Athlone Registration Club, £20 to the St Mary's chapel, £10 each to St Mary's convent, the poor of St Peter's, the poor of St Mary's and the Temperance Society and £5 each to St Mary's temperance society, the band, and St Peter's convent.[89] Furthermore, a petition from disgruntled conservative electors to the House of Commons suggests that Collett's largesse did not end there.[90] Twenty-seven named voters were alleged to have received bribes of between £5 and £15 each, and the Catholic clergy were alleged to have been instrumental in the disbursement of the money. Several of the recipients had previously been identified as tory voters suspected of taking bribes in the 1835 election, among whom was one James Roper a labourer who lived in Strand Street.[91] In testimony to the parliamentary select committee Roper told of being canvassed by Daniel H. Farrell who introduced Collett as a friend of his and 'a gentleman that would stand for the country and vote for Ireland'.[92] Several months later Rev. Kieran Kilroe called to Roper's house which was undergoing renovation, suggested that he should get the windows glazed and gave him a gift of £5 for that purpose.[93] This was a substantial donation since at this time the average labourer in the Athlone area might have expected to earn in the region of £7 a year.[94] Roper professed ignorance of the motive for the generosity but he allowed that he had been offered forty-five sovereigns by the 'other side' to vote for Beresford.[95] Another voter, Michael Curley, admitted to receiving £5 from Mr Farrell through Rev. Wallace, a curate in St Peter's parish.[96] Curley had been financially embarrassed and had approached Farrell for money. Farrell said he would 'be kind to him' in consequence of the previous election when Curley had voted for him. Both Curley and Roper denied the substance of a previous deposition in which they admitted receiving money to vote for Collett, and as a result the petition was withdrawn.

The significance of the election result was problematic in that everyone read their own implications into the Liberal victory. A letter writer suggested in the local newspaper that clergy and laity had united in 'a death struggle between their own and a rabid tory faction led by a Beresford, a name hateful to Irish ears', but a sceptical *Freeman's Journal* wondered why the people of Athlone should exult: 'the Liberals have earned a vote but no triumph'.[97]

Shortly after the electorate of the borough chose an English Liberal as its voice in parliament in the election of 1843, the wider public evinced a different political agenda when Athlone became the venue of a Repeal demonstration on Sunday 18 June 1843.[98] The establishment of a Precursor Society in the town to agitate for corporate reforms, the extension of the franchise and the abolition of tithes, had been the occasion of a 'numerous and respectable' meeting in 1838.[99] Large gatherings had also attended Repeal meetings at the end of 1842, but the demonstration of 1843 was undoubtedly of such proportions as to constitute the greatest peacetime assembly in the history of the town.[100] Daniel O'Connell had designated 1843 as 'the Repeal year' and to further this objective some forty outdoor rallies termed 'monster meetings' by *The Times*, were held, usually at strategically located country towns.[101] The spatial pattern of these meetings in the midland counties reveals a blanket coverage, with venues surrounding Athlone such as Longford, Mullingar, Tullamore, Nenagh, Loughrea, and Roscommon.[102] Athlone's nodal position gave it a large catchment area in Connacht and Leinster and drew an attendance estimated at about 200,000.[103]

The process was set in train when O'Connell was met on 14 May 1843 by a deputation from Athlone who presented him with an invitation to a public meeting and dinner for the purpose of forwarding the great cause of Ireland's rejuvenation.[104] The signatories included Lord Ffrench of Castlefrench County Galway, the Catholic bishops of Ardagh and Meath, Sir Michael Dillon Bellew of Mount Bellew, and various Athlone notables. The meeting was to be held at Summerhill House, the residence of Mr Edward Murphy located just west of Athlone. The night before the event O'Connell accepted Murphy's hospitality, and in the morning he made an entrance to Athlone where he gathered a multitude and led a procession back to the meeting place.[105] The focal points of O'Connell's progress through Athlone were the residences of Rev. O'Reilly in Repeal Street, and Rev. Kilroe in Gleeson Street, where he exchanged greetings with dignitaries and clergy of the respective parishes. The route was marked by numerous triumphal arches bearing legends such as 'men of Erin we struggle to regain our native parliament, all Europe and America are looking on' or 'we seek equality not ascendancy through Repeal'. The procession itself was a choreographed piece of street theatre with the participants arranged in a moving status pyramid. In the leading carriage was Edward Murphy, then came the carriages of O'Connell and Lord Ffrench, followed by three or four vehicles filled almost exclusively with ladies. Interspersed with the carriages were the trades, 'orderly and well dressed', each preceded by a band and carrying banners such as that of the coachmakers which bore the motto: 'a parliament at home, a home-made coach, no alien then could on our trade encroach'. Shoemakers, coach-makers, broguemakers, builders, victuallers, tailors and bakers lined up behind bands from Athlone and the neighbouring towns of Birr, Roscommon, Mullingar, Moate, Kilbeggan, Clara and Banagher.

Jacob Venedy, a German traveller and admirer of O'Connell, recorded his impressions of the events at Summerhill which he likened to a well played drama.[106] The visitor took his place on the main platform which was occupied by citizens of the middle classes, of whom every third man at least was a priest.[107] Alongside was a second stand erected to accommodate the ladies. Venedy was struck by the order or regulation with which the crowd involuntarily presented itself. At the front were the pedestrians, men and young lads, behind them horsemen in ranks and troops, further off lying on the ground, standing or walking about, were the women, the less strong, or the less curious. The men wore grey frieze coats which were the prevailing fashion, while the women dressed in scarlet presented a striking contrast. O'Connell in his discourse attacked whigs and tories alike, expressed his loyalty to the Queen, and indicated the advantages to be derived from Repeal, but the epiphany occurred when a runaway horse caused a panic to seize the crowd.[108] It was like the rapid advance of a heavy body of cavalry and Venedy was reminded that the garrison of Athlone had been considerably strengthened. All was rushing to confusion and disorder when the calm but thunderous tones of O'Connell came pealing over the multitude. He merely said 'stand still!' and all movement ceased. It was, wrote Venedy, 'as if fate would put the power of his word to the proof, and wish to demonstrate that it was omnipotent'.[109] It was this almost mechanical obedience that so alarmed O'Connell's enemies and led Venedy to conclude that 'in England they neither know the power of the man himself nor the character of the movement in which he is engaged'.[110]

The great assembly had galvanised the common people, the clergy, the middle classes, and even a few aristocrats for a common purpose and must have left a lasting impression on all participants. The soldiers in the garrison had crowded the walls of the fortress to watch the spectacle but there is little evidence to indicate the involvement of the Protestant population whose clergy and gentry noticeably go unmentioned in the newspaper coverage.[111] They may have shared the disapprobation of the English gentleman, resident near Athlone, who haughtily informed Herr Venedy that he had not crossed the bridge to view the spectacle, and declined any further discussion on the subject.[112]

The establishment of a Repeal reading room in Bastion Street in 1845 was intended to cement the involvement of the ordinary people in political activity.[113] Here the 'poor mechanic' had an opportunity of 'improving his knowledge of man and things', and 'men who had hitherto spent their time standing about the streets or carousing in whiskey shops, were now perceived to frequent the reading room with every appearance of enjoyment'.[114] Further Repeal demonstrations were held in 1844 and 1845, but when a Repeal candidate was offered to the electorate of the borough in 1847, they chose instead the Peelite William Keogh who, more than any other Athlone M.P. was to leave his mark on the national stage.[115]

Political developments, 1847–85

William Nicholas Keogh was the best known and most controversial member of parliament to represent the borough of Athlone in the nineteenth century. Keogh and his colleague John Sadleir, M.P. for Carlow, became objects of vilification at the end of 1852 for accepting government office and deserting the nascent Independent party, to which they had been pledged.[1] The subsequent extinction of that party made the defection of the two M.P.s seem even more momentous in retrospect. T.P. O'Connor M.P., a native of Athlone wrote that:

> Of all the men and forces that created Fenianism, Judge Keogh was the most potent. It was his treason that broke down all faith in constitutional agitation, and it was the want of faith in constitutional agitation that drove men to the desperate risks to life and liberty of a physical force movement.[2]

Keogh's colourful career is of intrinsic interest but his success in retaining his Athlone seat despite his notorious tergiversation shows how factors of personality and self interest could override national concerns in the minds of the electors.

In 1842 the Athlone Conservative party retained the Catholic barrister William Keogh to act on its behalf at the registration of voters.[3] In 1847 it was suggested to Keogh that the Conservative party would be disposed to support him as their candidate since he had relations in the area who would not have been prepared to support any other person holding similar views.[4] Keogh was born in Galway and educated in Dublin but his family came from Keoghville in South Roscommon.[5] The value of this connection became apparent when William Kelly, agent for the sitting Liberal M.P. John Collett, deserted to the Keogh camp just two months before the 1847 general election, on the grounds that Keogh was a near relation of his.[6] A week before the election Collett withdrew from the contest and the Right Reverend Dr Browne, bishop of Elphin, and the repealers of the district, selected a local distiller John O'Beirne as the Repeal candidate.[7] At Sunday mass on 1 August, Rev. Martin O'Reilly parish priest of St Peter's urged his congregation not to support Keogh, and he condemned Keogh's supporters.[8] After mass two of Keogh's friends, physician Dr William H. O'Connell, and pawnbroker Mr Patrick Keating, were attacked by some unruly members of the congregation, and Mr

Keating had to be given police protection.[9] At the nomination of candidates Bishop Browne criticised Keogh for his advocacy of the former viceroy De Grey and said that although he professed his Catholicity, he was only a Catholic in name.[10] Despite this opposition Keogh won the election by a margin of six votes.[11] The victory was ascribed by his opponents to the 'turpitude' of the twenty Catholics who voted for him and the twelve others who ran away.[12] O'Beirne lodged an appeal on the grounds of 'gross corruption by open and notorious bribery and treating' but the case was withdrawn, with the suspicion that a questionable deal had been arrived at.[13]

The reputation and popularity of Athlone's new M.P. increased dramatically in the next few years, a development epitomised by a banquet in Athlone at Rourke's hotel, held in his honour at the instigation of the electors of the borough on 28 October 1851.[14] The chair was taken by Rev. Martin O'Reilly, who was now an archdeacon, while the guests included the bishop of Elphin and the bishops of Meath and Clonfert. This change of attitude on the part of former critics had been effected partly by Keogh's prominent role in opposition to the Ecclesiastical Titles Bill introduced into parliament by Lord John Russell early in 1851. Keogh was the principal speaker at a mass meeting of Catholics held in Dublin in August 1851 to protest against the measure and was one of the founders of the Catholic Defence Association, established in consequence of it.[15] He also took part in the tenant right movement and was one of only two M.P.s to attend its inaugural conference held in Dublin in August 1850.[16] This too served to enhance Keogh's prestige and a great tenant right demonstration in Athlone in June 1852 attended by 10,000 people including the great bulk of the inhabitants of the town, became, in effect, an election rally to secure Keogh's return to parliament.[17] Another independent factor acting in his favour was the anti-Catholic riots in Stockport, Cheshire, blamed by Irish Catholics on a persecuting Conservative government.[18] Thus when Keogh, now an independent Liberal, stood against the Conservative R.B. Lawes in the general election of 1852 he had the backing of the Catholic clergy while retaining some Protestant support.[19] Having been proposed by Rev. O'Reilly and seconded by Netterville E. Abbott 'a highly respectable Protestant', Keogh won the election by the comfortable margin of eighty-seven votes to ten.[20] On the hustings Keogh remarked that he was opposed by a party who would not vote for any person for less than £60 a head, a contention that carries some weight, coming from the mouth of one who represented that party at the previous election.[21]

The new Conservative government of the fourteenth earl of Derby was defeated on its first budget and was replaced at the end of 1852 by a coalition of Liberals and Peelites.[22] Lord Aberdeen, a Peelite, became prime minister and among the office holders were William Keogh as solicitor general for Ireland, and John Sadleir as a lord of the treasury.[23] At once both men were violently attacked as pledge-breakers and renegades since they were understood to have committed themselves to remaining independent of the government.[24] At a banquet in Rourke's Hotel Athlone on 28 October 1851, attended by up to 200 people including the archbishop of Tuam, John McHale, Keogh had unambiguously declared 'I will not support any party which will not make it the first ingredient of its political existence to repeal the Ecclesiastical Titles Bill . . . '.[25] His acceptance of office gave great offence to the Irish Party and Gavan Duffy wrote in the *Nation* on 1 January 1853 that Keogh had gone into parliament fully pledged to the cause of tenant right, and the repeal of the Ecclesiastical Titles Bill, yet a month had not elapsed until he had 'dropped like a rotten plum' into the treasury.[26] Such was his unpopularity, according to the *Nation* that while driving through the streets of Dublin, his furtive eye seemed to anticipate the fall of a dead cat or a shower of rotten eggs.[27]

The gulf between national politics and the *realpolitik* of the local context was evident when Keogh returned to Rourke's Hotel on 9 January 1853 for the purpose of explaining the motives which induced him to accept office.[28] Keogh was received with great enthusiasm and his audience of electors expressed their satisfaction with the prudence and consistency of his acceptance of office. Paradoxically, the abandonment of his independent stance which made Keogh a national hate figure, was seen by his constituency as a mark in his favour, for a place in government gave access to the power of government patronage. These were the days before competitive entrance examinations and government posts were filled directly by the nomination of the minister concerned. When lesser posts became vacant the ministers tended to accept the recommendation of political friends and in particular of M.P.s on the government side of the house. Thus, in the words of one of Keogh's fiercest critics, the 'desperately needy voters' saw in a government official 'a man better able to bribe themselves and to obtain situations for their sons'.[29] The prospect of personal gain had an ecumenical appeal as instanced by 'a highly respectable Protestant tradesman' who summarised his political philosophy thus: 'I am a Protestant . . . and my father was a Protestant and his father before him, but the man I want to see returned for Athlone is the man that leaves the money in the town'.[30]

There was a saying in Athlone in Keogh's day that every young fellow who could or could not write his name, had obtained a place in the customs, or some other of the public departments.[31] In 1854 the 'corrupt committee' constituted for enquiry into corrupt practices at elections heard evidence of several such appointments.[32] Asked whether he had obtained an appointment for any of his opponents, Keogh replied 'certainly not'.[33] The fact that their M.P was regarded as a traitor in certain quarters is unlikely to have weighed heavily on the minds of Athlone voters who received or expected to receive the benefits of such patronage. Thus, political behaviour which might have appeared perverse or unpatriotic from a national perspective was regarded as perfectly rational and justified at a local level. Indeed early in 1853 the Liberal electors of Athlone reacted with indignation to the 'foul lying and slanderous assertions' of Messrs Gray of the *Freeman's Journal* and Lucas of the *Tablet* concerning alleged corruption in the borough.[34]

Keogh, having taken office, had to seek re-election. The contest in April 1853 was notable for the intimidating pressure applied to the electors, particularly the forty or so whose allegiance was doubtful.[35] The agent of Thomas Norton, Keogh's Liberal opponent was caught in the act of endeavouring to bribe a shopkeeper named Kelly, whereupon he was dragged into the street and kicked, cuffed and rolled about until he was coated with mud.[36] The solicitor general himself was looking out of the window of his hotel when his suspicions were aroused by the behaviour of a man named Green.[37] Keogh followed Green down the street towards the bridge and observed him speaking to one of his supporters, John Mannion. Believing that Green was seeking to influence the voter he charged him with doing so and had him placed in custody. Keogh's suspicions proved well founded as Mannion said that the prisoner had offered him £30 to vote for Norton, or £20 to go out of the way until after the election. So closely was the bridge watched by night that travellers wishing to cross from Connacht to the Leinster side of Athlone town and who were unwilling to expose themselves to the inspection of the 'bludgeon men' sitting around watchfires at each side of the bridge, were obliged to cross in boats and go round the outskirts of the town. Norton and his principal supporters could not make their appearance but they were 'groaned and hooted' at, and such was the bad feeling shown towards them that only the presence of the police prevented them from being molested by mobs organised by the agents of the solicitor general.[38] When the polling commenced crowds of men and women assembled at the approaches to the booth and engaged in 'cheering, hooting and groaning'.[39] In numerous cases they 'pelted obnoxious persons with gutter' and spat upon them.[40] Crucially, Keogh had retained the support of Bishop Browne, and in the end he emerged victorious with seventy-nine votes to Norton's forty.[41] The *Freeman's Journal* not unreasonably concluded that the contest had been one of personal ambition rather than political principle, when the heretofore implacable enemies emerged from the booth to promenade the town arm in arm, 'to the no small astonishment of the poor dupes of Athlone, who up to the *dénoument* imagined that the farce was deep tragedy.'[42]

The deliberate omission of the member for Athlone from the list of toasts at a banquet of the town commissioners early in 1855 was interpreted as an indication that Keogh had difficulties to contend with among his former staunch supporters.[43] However, on 7 March 1855 following his appointment to the position of attorney general for Ireland, Keogh was returned without opposition, having been proposed by Dr Browne, bishop of Elphin.[44] The following year Keogh's parliamentary career came to an end when he was appointed judge of the Court of Common Pleas in Ireland.[45] He went on to preside over many high profile cases including the trials of prominent fenians such as Luby, O'Leary, and O'Donovan Rossa in the 1860s.[46] On 30 September 1878 William Keogh died at Bingen in Germany having cut his throat.[47] Keogh's unique success in securing his return for Athlone on four successive occasions may be ascribed to several factors, chief among which are his astute harnessing of national issues, local connections, clerical assistance and his liberal use of political patronage. There was also heavy election expenditure for which it is hard to find a justifiable explanation. In the general election of 1847 for example, Keogh admitted to spending over £2,000 of his own money.[48] However, personal charisma should not be ignored when seeking to explain William Keogh's popularity with the Athlone electorate. His oratory was described by the *Nation* as 'a jumble of bog Latin and flatulent English', but his ability to enthral his audience was acknowledged even by his critics.[49] The intimidatory atmosphere of election contests also required from the candidates a degree of courage, and Keogh was known to march through the streets with absolute fearlessness when 'a perfect hailstorm of stones was flying against him and his supporters.'[50] Not the least of Keogh's attributes as a politician was his conviviality. A candidate at Dungarvan complained of how he was 'expected to imbibe large quantities of punch, day and night, with successive batches of electors' and how failure in this terrible duty would seriously imperil his popularity.[51] Keogh was a heavy drinker all his life and took to this duty with an abandon that evoked wonder.[52]

The by-election which followed William Keogh's appointment to the Court of Common Pleas in 1856 led to an unexpected Conservative victory which proved to be their last in the borough of Athlone. Little is known about the mechanism by which Conservative candidates were selected since in Athlone as elsewhere, the Conservatives conducted their proceedings behind closed doors, whereas the Liberals advertised their adoption meetings beforehand and welcomed the attendance of the press.[53] However, the primacy of the Handcock family is indisputable, since following the unsuccessful candidacy of Lord Castlemaine's nephew, Richard Handcock, in 1832, a member of that family was involved in the nomination of the Conservative candidate at each subsequent election contested by the party. The Handcocks had their own candidate in 1856 in the person of Captain the Honourable Henry Handcock. Captain Handcock, the youngest son of Lord Castlemaine was aged twenty-two and had recently returned from service in the Crimea.[54] The Conservatives were induced to enter the field when thirty-two Catholics signed a requisition calling on the captain to come forward as a candidate for the representation of the borough and promising their warmest support.[55] Up to that point a Liberal victory had seemed inevitable. The number of votes that could be polled was estimated at 160 of which 108 were Catholics and fifty-two Protestants.[56] The Conservative vote was thought to roughly equate with the number of Protestants (about fifty), therefore the defection of Catholics from the Liberal camp would prove decisive.[57] It is worth noting that six of these estranged Catholic electors had previously been identified in an election petition as the recipients of bribes.[58] Thus it is not inconceivable that the voters simply seized the opportunity presented to auction their votes to the highest bidder.

The Liberal candidate was a Catholic, John Ennis, later Sir John, of Ballinahown Court, County Westmeath. He was the only son of Andrew Ennis, 'one of the prince merchants of Dublin', and for many years treasurer to the O'Connell tribute.[59] John Ennis was a substantial landowner with 5,397 acres in 1856, which had increased to 9,362 acres by 1874.[60] He was also a prominent figure in the world of business having been twice a governor of the Bank of Ireland and chairman of the Midland Great Western Railway, and of the Dublin Steam Packet Company.[61]

During the election in April 1856 the town was crowded with the tenants of each candidate, a great proportion of whom were armed with sticks which they brandished in the air as they ran up and down the streets.[62] There was, however, no serious violence and Handcock's victory by eighty-two votes to seventy was followed by great rejoicing.[63] The election confirmed the pervasive influence of the Handcocks in the political life of Athlone. While allowance must be made for opportunism on the part of some of the electors, the invitation to Henry Handcock to come forward as a candidate, and the public reaction to his victory indicates that the family was still held in high esteem. The traditional loyalty to the Handcock family and respect for its *rôle* was sufficiently powerful, on this occasion, to transcend the vicissitudes of factional politics locally and nationally. However, the Handcock restoration was to be short lived.

In the general election of 1857 the ultra conservatives determined to vote against Captain Handcock in consequence of his voting in parliament in favour of the continuance of the Maynooth grant.[64] The published lists of voters names show that most of the Catholic 'liberals' returned to the fold on this occasion and voted for Ennis.[65] The result was that Ennis, who stood on an Independent Opposition ticket, had a comfortable victory by 100 votes to fifty.[66] However, John Ennis does not appear to have been a popular figure. An election ballad entitled 'Blinkin' Jack, the Mimber for Athlone', which was sung in the streets of Athlone and Moate in 1859, spitefully refers to Ennis as a 'pompous upstart hucksther'.[67] Ennis is criticised for his support of the Conservative Prime Minister 'the scorpion Derby' and his performance in parliament is belittled thus:

> He blathers here like Nayro, or some other grand nabob;
> But in the House of Commons, Boys, he doesn't stir his gob.

More revealing is an allusion to Ennis as a harsh landlord:

Who driv out strugglin tinnants, whose lives were always spint
In toil, night noon and morning, for to pay his double rint?

Herein may lie the reason for the novel and insidious form of corruption to
which Ennis resorted in order to secure electoral support. The essence of this
system of control was that Ennis, through certain trusted agents in the borough,
arranged that voters in any state of impecuniosity should be lent sums of
money on giving promissory notes as security for it. So long as the voter did
his duty by Ennis or his son, the money would not be demanded, but the debt
could be called in after the election if the desired outcome was not obtained.
The scheme was eventually exposed in the course of litigation in 1874 when,
following the defeat of the young Ennis in the general election of that year,
attempts were made to secure the repayment of a number of these 'loans'.[68]

Early in 1859 the Hon. Henry Handcock died at the age of twenty-five
while tiger hunting in India.[69] In the general election of that year John Ennis,
a Liberal again (having stood as an Independent in 1857), was opposed by Robert
Preston Bayley who received the nomination of Robert J. Handcock.[70] Political
affiliations were fluid in this period and the *Athlone Sentinel* was forced to
publish the following correction: 'Bayley intends to come forward, not as we
were incorrectly led to believe last week, as a Conservative, but as a Liberal'.[71]
Later the paper observed in the light of Bayley's anodyne election address, that
there was scarcely a Derbyite (Conservative) candidate in the country that 'does
not, in the present crisis profess to be a Liberal of the purest water'.[72] Bayley
was unsuccessful despite the expenditure of £5,000, receiving seventy-four
votes to 117 for Ennis.[73] This was not a contest of political principles and one
of Ennis's henchmen later gave a succinct explanation of the outcome: 'Mr.
Bayley offered £35 to each voter and Sir John gave £40 and was returned'.[74]

John Ennis admitted that money had been spent in bribery in the 1859
election but said that he was not aware of it until afterwards.[75] Mr James
Murtagh gave evidence that he had been engaged as an agent by Ennis in the
1859 election and that he had received a parcel of money 'about the size of his
hat' for distribution.[76] He did not think that Ennis would advance 2s. 6d. to
any man who had no vote. Two men in Murtagh's employment, Patrick Casey
and Thomas Carew Bracken, were engaged in the distribution of money to
the voters.[77] Patrick Casey told Moate Quarter Sessions he received £2,200
to spend on the 1859 election and spent it all at once. Voters got sums ranging
from £30 to £55.[78] Bracken gave evidence at Roscommon Quarter Sessions
of acting on behalf of John Ennis in lending money on bills.[79] Bracken recom-
mended people to Ennis who were desirous of money. He could not say that
he was an agent for Ennis, he was more an agent for the people.[80] Ennis had
been a 'bill discounter' in Athlone since 1832.[81] Bracken witnessed over 150
bills for persons in Athlone, but Ennis accepted only fifty or sixty of them as
the security offered was not sufficient.[82] When asked if he knew what prices

were given for votes in Athlone, Bracken deposed that 'they rose and fell according to the state of the market'.[83]

Ennis contended that these 'loans' were *bona-fide* mercantile transactions and claimed to have discounted bills for persons who had no votes, and for persons who voted against him.[84] Thus, after the 1874 election Sir John tried to get payment of his promissory notes through his land agent Thomas Quinn. In twenty-nine cases processes were issued and at Moate Quarter Sessions a test case was put before a jury.[85] The defendant was John Flannery who kept a grocery and provision shop in Mardyke Street, Athlone. Flannery had signed a promissory note for £30 on the understanding he claimed that he would not be asked to repay it. The question at issue was whether Sir John Ennis, a wealthy baronet, contemplated lending small sums of money in Athlone as a regular investment of his capital or whether the money was paid over for the purpose of corrupting and obtaining power over the voter. At this time Ennis had an estimated income of £16,000 per year and the jury considered it implausible that he should be involved in a 'miserable loan bank'.[86] It was found that the note was tainted with an illegal consideration and the case was decided in favour of the defendant.[87]

Ennis had neither the national profile nor the charisma of William Keogh, but he used his wealth to forge a barefaced cash relationship with the electors, one in which national issues and interests played little part. However, at this time, when the electors were motivated by immediate material considerations, Athlone also had associations with fenianism, a national movement which promised an alternative to the strong localism of mid-century parliamentary politics.

In addition to his activities as an 'agent for the people' in procuring money from Sir John Ennis, Thomas Carew Bracken had a simultaneous involvement with fenianism. On 17 February 1866 a bill was rushed through parliament permitting the indefinite detention of any person in Ireland on warrant of the lord lieutenant; this was followed by the arrest of hundreds of fenian suspects which wreaked havoc on fenianism in Ireland.[88] Henry Smith, the sub inspector of constabulary in Athlone, reported to Dublin Castle that the local magistrate and all the well disposed and loyal inhabitants of Athlone looked upon the arrest of Bracken on 29 March as one of the most important arrests to have been made in the town.[89] The arrest, he considered, had a visible effect on the people, since the impression among the lower classes had been that no person in Bracken's position could be touched.[90] Bracken was the brother in law of Patrick Carey, a Dublin hotel keeper, whose premises was the favourite resort of fenians and of Irish Americans.[91] Bracken himself had found lodgings in Athlone for Captain James Murphy, a deserter from the American army operating as a fenian agent, and the constabulary suspected that Bracken was acting as an ambassador between Captain Murphy and the brotherhood in Dublin.[92]

The first inkling of a fenian presence in the town was when a seditious placard appeared in February 1862 bearing the symbol of a harp, urging people to arm themselves with a rifle, and indicating that American help was on the way.[93] The resident magistrate, William Beckett, did not consider this to be a serious threat, viewing it rather as the production of 'some foolish mad person'.[94] The complacency of the authorities was shaken when in November 1864 a man named Patrick 'Pagan' O'Leary was arrested in Athlone on the evidence of some members of the garrison whom he had attempted to seduce from their allegiance.[95] Henceforth there was a heightened sensitivity with regard to the conduct of the army, and in particular, the soldiers' drinking habits were closely monitored. In March 1865 John Murphy was indicted at Mullingar assizes for having accosted a private in the 25th regiment, and having bought him drink in two public houses and attempted to swear him into the brotherhood.[96] The jury in this case failed to agree a verdict, thereby exemplifying the difficulty of securing a conviction by the normal legal process. Loose talk in another public house led to Corporal John Mulvey being summarily dispatched to the Curragh even though the informant was acknowledged as an unreliable witness.[97] The colonel commanding the Fifth Fusiliers prohibited his men from going into Martin Kennedy's public house in Queen Street which was suspected of being a fenian haunt.[98] Kennedy was one of nine alleged conspirators rounded up in a surprise raid on the night of 18 February 1866 following the suspension of *habeas corpus*.[99]

The government was not alone in its concern. Archdeacon O'Reilly denounced 'the insane movement of the fenians' from the altar, and instanced the case of Poland 'of whose recent melancholy history this deluded party seems to be forgetful'.[100] The people of Poland, he pointed out, had risen up believing they would be assisted by England, Austria, and France, but no aid came, and they were crushed. Fenian hopes of American aid would likewise be disappointed, the archdeacon told his parishioners, and he counselled that constitutional means were safest. The government action appears to have convinced the public of the wisdom of the archdeacon's assessment, for the constabulary considered the arrests to 'have had the salutary effect of checking the increase of members of the fenian conspiracy'.[101]

In Athlone, as elsewhere, clerical influence was an important element in the complex political equation throughout this period. At Kinsale, the parish priest and his curate 'controlled' thirty-four (or almost a quarter) of the votes, and individual priests had prevailing roles in Galway, Dungarvan, Tralee and other constituencies.[102] In the general election of 1865 the Catholic bishops and clergy made an orchestrated attempt to unseat John Ennis. Bishop Gillooly of Elphin was dissatisfied with the 'selfish, uncatholic, and unpatriotic' course pursued by Ennis in parliament, and specifically criticised his defiance of the church by his votes on the model school question.[103] The bishop was also disturbed by the bribery practised by Ennis's agents 'without any disguise or concealment', and his colleague, Bishop Kilduff of Ardagh and Clonmacnoise, felt it was their imperative duty to rescue the borough from its current 'state of degradation and venality, so odious and so shameful'.[104] Ennis' rival for the

Liberal vote was Denis J. Reardon, a Catholic gentleman from London who offered himself to the electorate as a liberal Conservative disposed to give a fair and legitimate support to Lord Derby, and to vote against the Whigs should an opportunity occur of placing his party in power.[105]

Bishop Kilduff wrote to his colleague Bishop Gillooly urging him to send 'the strongest letter he could pen' to Archdeacon O'Reillly in support of Reardon, and promising to write a similar letter to the priests of St Mary's parish notwithstanding that he had already done his best by verbal exhortation.[106] Bishop Gillooly acted immediately and requested the archdeacon and his clergy to unite with the clergy of St Mary's parish and to use every lawful exertion to secure the return of Reardon.[107] However, even the most explicit clerical endorsement did not ensure a unanimous Catholic response. There was a remarkable instance of open defiance on 13 July 1865, when Martin Carroll the pawnbroker, castigated Archdeacon O'Reilly at the hustings 'in the most unmeasured terms' for connecting himself with the Protestant party to defeat Ennis.[108] The archdeacon told the electors that Reardon was a far better candidate than Ennis, who although he had a large property in the next county never spent as much as sixpence in the town.[109] At this point Carroll began to wave his hat and urged on Ennis's tenantry and a crowd of his supporters to shout. Tin cans filled with stones and powder flasks filled with shot were rattled to drown the speaker's voice. O'Reilly could not be heard and the cordons of constabulary had to fix bayonets to restore order. Upon leaving the hustings Carroll was followed by a number of boys and women who assailed him with stones and mud, and he was forced to seek shelter in the Prince of Wales Hotel in Church Street. After nightfall, a large mob attacked Carroll's home in Connaught Street and soon demolished the windows and everything that a stone could reach. His pawn offices in Church Street, Barrack Street and Mardyke Street were also damaged. The published voting lists reveal that Carroll wisely refrained from voting in the election.[110] Archdeacon O'Reilly claimed that the Catholic voters in his parish unanimously refused to vote for Ennis due to the insult offered to him through Carroll.[111]

The subtle deployment of episcopal power behind the scenes may have had an even greater impact on the course of this election than the overt activities of the clergy. Of especial importance was a promise elicited by Bishop Kilduff from his old friend and school fellow, James Murtagh, to support any candidate who enjoyed his recommendation, and that of the bishop of Elphin.[112] Kilduff immediately wrote to his colleague recommending him to visit Murtagh in order to cement the arrangement.[113] It was Murtagh's employees who were involved in the distribution of 'loans' to voters in 1859 and his role as power broker was recognised by Bishop Kilduff when he wrote: 'I do not attach so much value to the six votes the Murtagh's have in the boro' as I do to the painful influence they have over their customers and creditors, the publicans and bankers of Athlone.'[114] The potential of this influence may be guessed at from the extensive business interests controlled by the Murtagh family who operated as millers, corn merchants, tea and spirit dealers, and canal boat proprietors at Athlone, Ballykeeran Mills, Ballymahon, Carrick on Shannon, Cavan, Galway, Longford Mills, Mullingar, Sligo, Shrule Mills, Tobber Mills, Moyvore and at Eden Quay in Dublin.[115] The master of the Ranelagh school, Joseph McNamara, for example, had been pressurised by Murtagh not to vote for Bayley, the Conservative candidate who opposed Ennis in 1859, because, he admitted 'I placed myself under heavy obligation in getting him to become security for one of my sons to the amount of £1,000.'[116] In 1865, now that Murtagh had been detached from the Ennis camp, McNamara was free to vote for the Conservative, George Handcock.[117] Reardon, the favourite of the Catholic clergy, won the election comfortably with 107 votes, more than the combined total of Ennis and Handcock. Ironically, given the episcopal stance on corruption, it was later claimed that Reardon's election was 'remarkable for its dishonesty', and that 'his intellect failed, believed to be caused by his pecuniary losses'.[118] Sir John Ennis, however, was in no doubt as to the pivotal role of the Catholic clergy in determining the outcome of the election. The following year he was said to be oblivious to the voters, being satisfied that he would regain his former position through the same influence that deprived him of it; the bishops of Ardagh and Elphin.[119]

The issue of disestablishment dominated the 1868 general election. The identity of view which prevailed between Gladstone and the Catholic clergy resulted in the influence of the Catholic church being brought to bear on the Liberal side throughout the country.[120] The candidates' efforts to curry favour with the church were the cause of some amusement. Sir John Ennis was noted as a regular attender of his parish chapel, where on one Sunday, he and his son each gave £1 at the collection.[121] Another potential candidate in the congregation had the presence of mind to outbid his antagonist by leaving down £5, leading a newspaper editorial to express regret that elections did not take place once a year in Athlone.[122]

In the event Sir John Ennis allowed his son, John James, to stand in his stead, because, a few days before the election he gave a man £30 on a promissory note and he had legal advice that this might invalidate his election.[123] Ennis was opposed by another Liberal, John Staniforth, and by Robert Preston Bayley who had contested the 1859 election.[124] Bayley, a Conservative, though reluctant to be described as such, did not publish an election address, and at the nominations he had barely announced his intentions to enter parliament 'free and unpledged' when he was shouted down by the assembled crowd.[125]

It is doubtful if the minds of Athlone voters were greatly exercised by disestablishment or any other national issue. Before the election one voter, John Cullen, went to see Ennis's agent, Mr Bracken, who told him that he believed 'their side would have the most money', but that he did not think that it would exceed £20 or £30. Cullen voted for John Ennis and after the election walked to Ballinahown with the bill that Bracken had given him. Sir John gave him a glass of whiskey and the money was sent to him afterwards. Another voter, James Curley, testified at Roscommon Quarter Sessions that in the 1868 election 'proposals were held out on both sides' and he decided to vote for Ennis. He went to Ballinahown and told Sir John that he was going to America as he had got into difficulties. Sir John gave him a cheque for £50. On being asked if that £50 had any connection with the election he replied amidst laughter, 'it helped the cause; if I had not a vote I would not have gone near him, as I could not expect him to be so generous.'[126] The generosity of Sir John was in all probability the main factor in determining the election result. John Ennis was returned with 154 votes to 111 for Bayley and only one vote for Staniforth.[127]

The year 1874 saw the first in a series of historic Irish electoral contests of which home rule was the central issue.[128] In Athlone a meeting under the chairmanship of Bishop Gillooly endorsed Edward Sheil as the home rule candidate to oppose John Ennis, following an unsuccessful attempt by the persistent R.P. Bayley to garner support.[129] Sheil, from London, was the nephew of Richard Lalor Sheil founder member of the Catholic Association.[130] Ennis was attacked for his 'vague, ambiguous and unsatisfactory' declarations on home rule and denominational education and for his complete failure to mention amnesty for fenian prisoners in his election address.[131] A feeble measure to extend the franchise in 1868 had reduced the poor rate qualification from £8 to 'over £4' for rated occupiers, and granted the vote for the first time to lodgers.[132] This merely increased the electorate of the borough from 318 in 1868 to 351 in 1874.[133] A much more significant departure was the introduction of secret voting in 1872, although for a time few were entirely convinced that men of influence might not somehow penetrate the veil of secrecy.[134] Sheil and Ennis emerged from the polling tied on 140 votes each but the inexpertise of the voters led the sheriff to reject a further thirty-five ballot papers or 11 per cent of the total.[135] Later on appeal, the Court of Common Pleas ruled that some of these votes were valid and that the poll should be amended to 153 for Sheil and 148 for Ennis.[136]

The rematch between Sheil and Ennis in 1880 is better documented for the reason that the narrow margin of Ennis's victory (163 votes to 162), led Sheil to undertake a petition to parliament, with the financial backing of the Land League.[137] The petition unearthed further evidence of how the franchise was used to profitable effect. William Rezin came from Edinburgh to vote for Ennis, at the request of Church Street draper, William Burgess, who subsequently gave him employment.[138] Rev. Robert Foster, a Protestant chaplain at the Royal Military School, was likewise prompted to travel from Downpatrick when he received a letter from an Ennis supporter containing a cheque for £3 travelling expenses. J.P. Foy offered Robert Gladstone the management of one of his business houses if he voted for Sheil, and told Gladstone to 'think of Fatherland and Nationality'. However, Gladstone testified at the inquiry into the election petition that he voted for Ennis, as he had done for the family since 1859, without fee or payment. William Kelly, town clerk and solicitor for the Ennis family, called on Rev. Dr Michael Coffey, parish priest of St Peter's, and suggested that a new church might be one of the beneficial consequences of Ennis's return for the borough.[139] Kelly himself had received £300 to act as Ennis's agent in 1868 but denied accepting a retainer for his work in 1880.[140] Netterville Abbot was indifferent as to which of the candidates succeeded but decided for Ennis when William Kelly's son John Charles paid £65 for the use of his house for election purposes.[141] Meanwhile other voters continued to be bound by promissory notes, although Kieran Cosgrave admitted to voting for Sheil despite the fear of being asked to repay his bill to Ennis.[142]

While the ideological motivation of the electors may be suspect, views were passionately held and voters were under pressure from a variety of quarters. Upwards of 3,000 people attended an election rally in Castle Street on 24 March 1880 when they heard Charles Stewart Parnell describe Ennis as 'a West British whig'. Rev. John Pyne, a curate in St Peter's parish, told the assembly that Ennis was 'morally and physically unfit to represent Athlone' and that he 'relied on his money bags and the Orangemen of the town for his election'.[143] Rev. Pyne said the gospel of the week (it was Holy Week), reminded him of Sir John Ennis's supporters. They were, he claimed, like Judas Iscariot and as such, he predicted that they would meet the fate of Judas Iscariot. After the meeting a large stone was thrown at Sir John and windows were broken in his election headquarters and in the office of his solicitor. Rev. Pyne was accused of exerting an undue influence on his parishioners, but the judges at the trial of the election petition merely remarked that the presence of a clergyman watching his flock at the polling together with an 'enormous number of personation agents' could seriously affect the secrecy and the whole purpose of the Ballot Act.[144] It was concluded that the priest had taken a very active part in the election and that he had to a certain extent mixed up election matters with his duties as a clergyman. This was the mildest of censures considering that when Rev. Pyne was called to the death bed of a man who had voted for Ennis, the priest asked the dying man why he had not sent for Ennis.[145] In the case of another voter Rev. Pyne's influence was outweighed by pressure from neighbours. When Rev. Pyne called to canvass John McNamara of Golden Island he was told that Mr McNamara would do as his neighbours did. Mr McNamara later admitted that he had voted because one of his neighbours James Curley 'made him vote'. There was a suggestion that the voters of Golden Island had been bribed by Ennis and counsel at the trial of the election petition quipped that the place had never better title to the name than during election week.[146]

The 1880 election occurred at a time of intense distress in the hinterland of Athlone. Falling agricultural prices and the almost total failure of the potato crop, due to blight, in 1879 and again in 1880 caused serious hardship and left an estimated 800 people in distress in St Peter's parish and a further 935 in St Mary's parish. Despite relief measures there were still some 300 distressed persons in the Athlone area in 1880.[147] On 7 November 1880 a great demonstration in sympathy with the land movement was held in Athlone.[148] The assembled thousands heard Parnell call upon the government to imitate the king of Prussia in 1813, who was not afraid to give the land to his people. The urban population were active participants in this campaign for land reform. Among the many banners at the demonstration was one which bore the slogan 'Shannon Sawmills men warmly sympathetic with the Land League'. After the public meeting J.P. Foy proposed the formation of a committee for the purpose of calling a meeting of the traders of Athlone and the farmers of the vicinity in order to form a branch of the National Land League.[149]

The urban members of the League were available when required to mobilise at attempted evictions such as that of Mrs Kearney near Ballykeeran, a tenant of Lord Castlemaine.[150] Alternatively the action was sometimes brought into the town itself as when over 1,000 people demonstrated against the sale of cattle seized from a Mrs Kilduff of Bushfield, another of Castlemaine's tenants.[151] Athlone also had its branch of the Ladies Land League with Mary Geoghegan, proprietor of the Prince of Wales hotel as president.[152] Dr Woodlock, bishop of Ardagh and Clonmacnoise warned women from taking part in public meetings but his words went unheeded.[153] Miss Mary O'Connor, sister to T.P. O'Connor, M.P., was charged at Athlone Petty Sessions on 12 March 1882 with having in a speech delivered at Drum incited to the non-payment of rent.[154] Two of the three magistrates present decided that Miss O'Connor should find bail for her good behaviour or be imprisoned for six months. The lady took the latter alternative and served nine weeks in Mullingar gaol.[155]

The death of Sir John James Ennis in 1884 left the borough seat vacant once more.[156] A high powered delegation of Irish Parliamentary Party M.P.s came to Athlone to promote the candidacy of Justin H. McCarthy. T.D. Sullivan, M.P., told a meeting in the Market Square that the time had come for Athlone to 'redeem the past' and take her place with the other Nationalist constituencies. Tim Healy said there were rumours of opposition and some persons 'almost hoped to resurrect the bones of Billy Keogh' but the people of Athlone now had a chance of wiping out the stains from their historic town.[157] In fact an attempt was made to induce a candidate to stand in the Liberal interest. The O'Connor Don, described by Parnell as 'a sample of West Britishism in Ireland', was assured of seventy Liberal votes, but he declined the nomination as did Major D'Arcy.[158] Sir John left no male heir and in the end the seat went to McCarthy without opposition. McCarthy's career as the parliamentary representative for Athlone came to a premature end in 1885 when the borough was closed. His last act was to give the vote of Athlone in the overthrow of the Gladstone government as the 'worst government that has ever misgoverned and misruled Ireland.'[159] Athlone was now incorporated in the constituencies of South Roscommon and South Westmeath, until 1899, when both the west town and the east town became part of South Westmeath constituency.[160]

The period from 1830 to 1885 began with the Protestant Conservative interest in a controlling position in the borough of Athlone but ended with its political role greatly reduced. The uncontested parliamentary elections before 1830 cannot have signified much to the general population but the extension of the franchise in 1832 ensured that subsequent elections were seldom lacking in excitement. The behaviour of the voters however, belied the campaign rhetoric and self interest largely prevailed over national concerns. It was said that 'the very whisper of a dissolution sent a visible thrill through the town, and the prospect of common gain swallowed up amid the people all other passions, religious and political, and united ordinarily discordant forces in amity and brotherhood'.[161] Thus the dramatic political changes of the period must be seen in the context of the mercenary calculations of a small electorate which fully warranted Athlone's designation as a rotten borough.

Conclusion

In terms of its size and population Athlone in 1885 did not differ greatly from the town of 1830. However, as this study has shown this was a period of considerable social change. The rapid pre-Famine population growth gave way to forty years of slow decline with attendant stagnation in trade and commerce. At the same time, improved communications were instrumental in the emergence of Athlone as a modern industrial town. The system of primary education was transformed, and tentative developments took place in intermediate education. There was also change in the field of local government when the regressive and unpopular corporation was abolished in 1840 and replaced by a body of elected town commissioners who effected a number of infrastructural improvements.

The political community has been singled out for examination in an effort to uncover something of the concerns and behaviour of the inhabitants of Athlone. Until the Irish Reform Act of 1832, the borough was under the effective control of Lord Castlemaine who resided at nearby Moydrum. The freemen voters remained solidly conservative but the enfranchisement of Catholics who occupied houses worth at least £2 a year resulted in a Liberal victory in the general election of that year. At the next election in 1835 the Conservative candidate, Captain George Mathew, resorted to the expedient of bribing sufficient voters to tilt the balance. This became the pattern in subsequent elections and Athlone became known as a 'rotten borough'. Mercenary voters attracted carpetbagging candidates to whom party labels were little more than flags of convenience. The career of William Keogh, Athlone's best known and most charismatic M.P. exemplifies how both the electorate and their representative were prepared to allow self-interest to override national concerns. Cynicism reached an even higher plane when Sir John Ennis and his son, John James, issued 'loans' to voters which they did not have to repay so long as the desired electoral outcome was forthcoming.

Corruption was one of the main factors in determining the nature of political conduct in Athlone but there were many other influences at work. Denominational affiliation was a key shaper and indicator of electoral choice and throughout the period the Catholic clergy were active persuaders on behalf of Liberal candidates while the family of Lord Castlemaine steadfastly backed Conservative candidates. As was the case in most local communities throughout Ireland at this time, electors were subject to pressures from a variety of other sources: family, neighbours, and men of wealth and influence, such as James Murtagh.[1] There was also, at election time, the threat or actuality of violence from unruly mobs which could on occasion include non electors from outside the town.

Athlone was by no means unique in respect of the turpitude of its political community. Carlow was up for sale to the highest bidder in the 1840s, and there is evidence of corrupt practice in Sligo, Cashel, Dungarvan, Coleraine, Clonmel, Carrickfergus and Youghal.[2] The *Nation* estimated that in 1859 twenty-seven of the thirty-three boroughs were significantly corrupt.[3] T.P. O'Connor M.P. defended his native Athlone saying it was neither better nor worse than the majority of Irish or English constituencies in that period.[4] He explained that the venality of the electorate was due to the dependence of *declassé* voters on the periodic electoral windfall and that for many 'the bribe entered into the whole economy of their poor, shrivelled squalid and weary lives'.[5] It is undoubtedly the case that the small size of the electorate, the nature of its religious balance, and the fact that there was no one proprietor with a controlling interest in the town, left the town vulnerable to political predators.

In the national context Athlone fared relatively well in the nineteenth century. While Athlone suffered a 15 per cent decline in population between 1841 and 1891 the population of the country as a whole fell by more than 40 per cent in the same period, and the neighbouring towns of Longford, Tullamore, Parsonstown, Moate, and Roscommon experienced reductions in population ranging from 23 per cent to 40 per cent.[6] A modest improvement in Athlone's status is indicated by its rise from thirty-seventh position in the urban hierarchy in rank order of size in 1841, to thirty-first place in 1891.[7] The strategic location of the town enabled Athlone to retain its large military garrison in the nineteenth century and to benefit from improvements in communications which, together with advances in the areas of local government and education, served to enhance the general welfare of its inhabitants as the century wore on.

Appendix 1
Athlone Elections, 1830–84

Year	Candidates	Political Affiliation	Votes Polled
1830	Richard Handcock	Conservative	37
	James Talbot	Liberal	2
1831	Richard Handcock	Conservative	33
	James Talbot	Liberal	3
1832	James Talbot	Liberal	125
	Richard Handcock	Conservative	104
1835	Capt. G.B. Mathew	Conservative	96
	James Talbot	Liberal	83
1837	John O'Connell	Liberal (Repealer)	
1841	G. de la P. Beresford	Conservative	30
	D.H. Farrell	Liberal	17
1843	John Collett	Liberal	114
	G. de la P. Beresford	Conservative	108
1847	William Keogh	Peelite	101
	J.L.M. O'Beirne	Repealer	95
1852	William Keogh, Q,C.	Liberal (Independent)	87
	R.B. Lawes	Conservative	10
1853	William Keogh, Q.C.	Liberal	79
	Thomas Norton	Liberal	40
1855	William Keogh, Q.C.	Liberal	
1856	Capt. Hon. Henry Handcock	Conservative	82
	J. Ennis	Liberal	70

(Appendix 1 continued)

Year	Candidates	Political Affiliation	Votes Polled
1857	J. Ennis	Independent Opposition	100
	Capt. Hon. Henry Handcock	Conservative	50
1859	J. Ennis	Liberal	117
	R.P. Bayley	Conservative	74
1865	D.J. Rearden	Liberal	107
	J. Ennis	Liberal	60
	Hon. George Handcock	Conservative	21
1868	J.J. Ennis	Liberal	154
	R.P. Bayley	Conservative	111
	John Staniforth	Liberal	1
1874	Edward Sheil	Home Ruler	140
	J.J. Ennis	Liberal	140
1880	Sir J.J. Ennis, bt	Liberal	163
	Edward Sheil	Home Ruler	162
1884	J.H. McCarthy	Home Ruler	

Sources: *Freeman's Journal* 1830–84; Brian M. Walker, (ed.), *Parliamentary election results in Ireland, 1801-1902* (Dublin, 1978), pp 197-252.

Appendix 2
Seats won at General Elections, 1832–80, by Parties

Changes resulting from petitions, or from by-elections following petitions, after general elections are shown in brackets.

	GENERAL ELECTIONS					
Parties	1832 (Dec.)	1835 (Jan.)	1837 (July-Aug.)	1841 (July)	1847 (Aug.)	1852 (July)
Conservatives	30	37(39)	32(34)	43(40)	31(30)	40
Peelites	—	—	—	—	11	2
Liberals	33(35)	34	43(40)	42(47)	25(27)	15(16)
Liberal Repealers	—	34(32)	30(31)	—	—	—
Liberal Independents	—	—	—	—	—	48(47)
Repealers	42(39)	—	—	20(18)	36(35)	—
Confederates	—	—	—	—	2(2)	—
Total	**105(104)**	**105**	**105**	**105**	**105**	**105**

	GENERAL ELECTIONS					
Parties	1857 (Mar-Apr.)	1859 (May)	1865 (July)	1868 (Nov.)	1874 (Feb.)	1880 (Mar-Apr.)
Conservatives	44(46)	55(54)	47	39(37)	33	25
Liberals	48(47)	50(51)	58	66	10	15
Independent Opposition	13(12)	—	—	—	—	—
Home Rulers	—	—	—	—	60	36
Home Rule Parnellites	—	—	—	—	—	27
Total	**105**	**105**	**105**	**105(103)**	**103**	**103**

Source: Brian M. Walker (ed.), *Parliamentary election results in Ireland, 1801–1922* (Dublin, 1978), p. 193.

Notes

ABBREVIATIONS

A.B.L.   Athlone Branch Library
D.N.B.   *Dictionary of National Biography*
F.J.   *Freeman's Journal*
H.C.   House of Commons
N.A.   National Archives
N.L.I.   National Library of Ireland
T.C.D.   Trinity College Dublin.

INTRODUCTION

1   *F.J.*, 10 Oct. 1885.
2   Brian M. Walker (ed.), *Parliamentary election results in Ireland, 1801–1922* (Dublin, 1978), p. 197; Peter Jupp, 'Urban politics in Ireland 1801–1831' in David Harkness, and Mary O'Dowd, (eds.), *The town in Ireland, Historical Studies xiii* (Belfast, 1981), p. 103.
3   K. Theodore Hoppen, *Elections, politics and society in Ireland, 1832–1885* (Oxford, 1984), p. 87; Harman Murtagh, *Irish Historic Towns Atlas: No. 6 Athlone* (Dublin, 1994), p. 7.
4   Hoppen, *Elections, politics and society in Ireland, 1832–1885*.
5   John B. O'Brien, 'Population, politics and society in Cork, 1780–1900' in Patrick O'Flanagan and Cornelius Buttimer (eds), *Cork: history and society: interdisciplinary essays on the history of an Irish county* (Dublin, 1993), pp 699–717; Ann Barry and Theodore Hoppen, 'Borough politics in O'Connellite Ireland: the Youghal poll books of 1835 and 1837' in *Journal of the Cork Historical and Archaeological Society,*

lxxxiii (1978), pp 106–46, and lxxxiv (1979), pp 15–43; Stephen A. Royle, 'The Lisburn by-elections of 1863' in *Irish Historical Studies*, xxv, no. 99 (May 1987), pp 277–91.
6   R.V. Comerford, 'Tipperary representation at Westminster, 1801–1918' in William Nolan (ed.), *Tipperary: history and society: interdisciplinary essays on the history of an Irish county* (Dublin, 1985), pp 325–38.
7   Patrick H. Murtagh, 'Tudor, Stuart and Georgian Athlone' (Ph.D. Thesis, University College, Galway. 1986).
8   Murtagh, *Irish Historic Towns Atlas*, pp 1–6.
9   Harman Murtagh (ed.), *Irish midland studies: essays in commeration of N.W. English* (Athlone, 1980); Marian Keaney and Gearóid O'Brien (eds), *Athlone bridging the centuries* (Mullingar, 1991).
10 The Moran Manuscripts: a collection of materials copied from various printed sources, mainly newspapers, relating to the history of Athlone and surrounding area, *c.* 1690–1899

compiled by Malachy Moran.
(N.L.I., MSS 1543–7).

ATHLONE AND ITS CHANGING
SOCIAL STRUCTURE, 1830–85

1 Murtagh, *Irish Historic Towns Atlas*, p. 7.
2 Murtagh, 'Tudor, Stuart and
   Georgian Athlone', p. 373.
3 An exception is the flattering
   account given in Mary Banim, *Here
   and there through Ireland* (Dublin,
   1891), pp 183–255.
4 Isaac Weld, *Statistical survey of the
   County of Roscommon* (Dublin,
   1832), p. 547.
5 Weld, *Statistical survey of the County
   of Roscommon*, p. 547.
6 Weld, *Statistical survey of the County
   of Roscommon*, p. 548.
7 H.D. Inglis, *Ireland in 1834. A journey
   through Ireland during the spring,
   summer and autumn of 1834* (2 vols,
   London, 1834), i, p. 192.
8 Leitch Ritchie, *Ireland, picturesque
   and romantic* (London, 1838), p. 181.
9 'The memoirs of Rosabel
   Langrishe' (two notebooks),
   (A.B.L., i, p. 18).
10 Ritchie, *Ireland, picturesque and
   romantic*, p. 179.
11 Ruth Delaney, 'Athlone navigation
   works, 1757–1849' in Harman
   Murtagh (ed.) *Irish midland studies*
   (Athlone, 1980), p. 201.
12 P.J. Currivan 'Athlone as a railway
   centre' in *Journal of the Irish Railway
   Record Society*, iv (1955–7), p. 210;
   Murtagh, *Irish Historic Towns Atlas*, p.4.
13 'Visitor's impression of Athlone,
   1852' in *Journal of the Old Athlone
   Society*, ii, no. 5 (1978), p. 76.
14 *General valuation of rateable property in
   Ireland, Athlone Union, County
   Westmeath* (Dublin, 1854),
   pp 89–111; *General valuation of
   rateable property in Ireland, Athlone
   Union, County Roscommon* (Dublin,
   1855), pp 26–48.

15 *Report of the local government and
   taxation of towns inquiry commission
   (Ireland), Pt iv: minutes of evidence*,
   pp 204–11, [C1696], H.C. 1877,
   xxxix, 213–19.
16 *Local government and taxation of towns
   report, minutes of evidence*, p. 203,
   [C1696], H.C. 1877, xxxix, 216.
17 Murtagh, *Irish Historic Towns Atlas*,
   p. 2.
18 Jeremiah Sheehan, *South Westmeath
   farm and folk* (Dublin, 1978), p. 46.
19 James Fraser, *A handbook for travellers
   in Ireland* (Dublin, 1844), p. 359.
20 *Population of counties in Ireland, 1831*,
   pp 96–7, pp 324–5, H.C. 1833,
   (254), xxxix. *Report of the
   commissioners appointed to take the
   census of Ireland for the year 1841*, pp
   116–7, pp 406–7, [504], H.C. 1843,
   xxiv. *The census of Ireland for the year
   1851, pt i: showing the area, population,
   and number of houses by townslands
   and electoral divisions, vol.i, province of
   Leinster*, p. 260, [1465, 1553, 1481,
   1486, 1488, 1492, 1503, 1496, 1502,
   1564, 1527, 1544], H.C. 1852–3, xci,
   vol. iv, province of Connacht, p. 184,
   [1557, 1548, 1542, 1555, 1560], H.C.
   1852–53, xcii. *The census of Ireland for
   the year 1861, pt i: showing the area,
   population, and number of houses by
   townslands and electoral divisions, vol. i,
   province of Leinster vol iv, province of
   Connacht, and summary of Ireland*,
   pp 420–1, pp 100–1, [3204], H.C.
   1863, lv. *Census of Ireland, 1871, pt i:
   area, houses and population; also the
   ages, civil conditions, occupations,
   birthplaces, religion, and education of the
   people, vol i, province of Leinster, with
   summary tables and indexes*, p. 370,
   [C662–1 to XIII], H.C. 1872, lxvii;
   *vol. iv, province of Connacht with
   summary tables for Ireland*, p. 437,
   [C1106–I to VII], H.C. 1874, lxxiv,
   pt ii. *Census of Ireland, 1881, pt i: area,
   houses and population; also the ages,
   civil or conjugal condition, occupations*,

birthplaces, religion, and education of the people, vol i, province of Leinster, p. 870, [C3042], H.C. 1881, xcvii; vol. iv, province of Connacht, p. 437, [C3268], H.C. 1882, lxxix. Census of Ireland, 1891, pt i: area, houses and population; also the ages, civil or conjugal condition, occupations, birthplaces, religion, and education of the people, for each county; with summary tables and indexes, vol i, province of Leinster, p. 870, [C6515], H.C. 1890–1, xcv; vol. iv, province of Connacht, p. 437, [C6685], H.C. 1892, xciii.

21   Parliamentary representation: boundary reports (Ireland), p. 5, H.C. 1831–2, (519), xliii, 21.

22   Murtagh, Irish Historic Towns Atlas, p. 7.

23   Parliamentary representation: boundary reports (Ireland), p. 7, H.C. 1831–2, (519), xliii, 23.

24   Report of the commissioners appointed to take the census of Ireland for the year 1841, p. viii, [505], H.C. 1843, xxiv.

25   Murtagh, 'Tudor, Stuart and Georgian Athlone', p. 316.

26   E.A. Wrigley, 'Eighteenth-century population growth' in E.A. Wrigley (ed.), People, cities and wealth (Oxford, 1987), pp 228–30.

27   Murtagh, 'Tudor Stuart and Georgian Athlone', p. 342.

28   Parliamentary gazetteer of Ireland (3 vols, London, 1846), i, p. 96.

29   Samuel Lewis, A topographical dictionary of Ireland (2 vols with atlas, London, 1837), i, p. 87.

30   Poor Inquiry (Ireland) Appendix D, p. 31, H.C. 1836, [36], xxxi, 147.

31   Weld, Statistical survey of the County Roscommon, p. 555.

32   Pigot and Co's City of Dublin and Hibernian provincial directory (Manchester and London, 1824), p. 129; Slater's National commercial directory of Ireland (Manchester, 1846), p. 6.

33   Pigot's directory 1824, p. 129; Slater's directory 1846, p. 5; Slater's directory 1856, p. 6; Slater's directory 1870, p. 11; Slater's directory 1881, p. 331; Slater's Royal commercial directory of Ireland (Manchester, 1894), p. 18.

34   Pigot's directory 1824, pp 128–30; Slater's directory 1894, pp 16–19.

35   Census of Ireland 1871 pt i: vol. i, province of Leinster, pp 822–925, [C662–i to xiii], H.C. 1872, lxvii, vol. iv province of Connacht, pp 496–501, [C1106–i to vii], H.C. 1874, lxxiv, pt.ii; Census of Ireland, 1881, pt. i: vol. i, province of Leinster, pp 922–6, [C3042], H.C. 1881, lcvii; vol. iv, province of Connacht, pp 407–503, [C3268], H.C. 1882, lxxix; Census of Ireland, 1891 pt. i: vol. i province of Leinster, pp 922–6, [C515], H.C. 1890–91, xcv; vol. iv; province of Connacht, pp 497–503, [C6685], H.C. 1892, xciii.

36   The classification of occupations is based on W.A. Armstrong, 'The use of information about occupation – an industrial classification' in E.A. Wrigley (ed.), Nineteenth-century society: essays in the use of quantitative methods for the study of social data (Cambridge, 1972), pp 215–310.

37   Mary Banim, Here and there through Ireland (Dublin, 1891), p. 204.

38   Minutes of evidence taken before the select committee on industries (Ireland), p. 347, H.C. 1884–5, (288), ix, 365.

39   Select committee on industries (Ireland), Appendix no.12 p. 750, H.C. 1884–85, (288), ix, 768.

40   Select committee on industries (Ireland), Appendix no.12 p. 750, H.C. 1884–85, (288), ix, 768.

41   Select committee on industries (Ireland), Appendix no.12 p. 750, H.C. 1884–85, (288), ix, 768.

42   Select committee on industries (Ireland), Appendix no.12 p. 750, H.C. 1884–85, (288), ix, 768.

43 *Select committee on industries (Ireland)*, Appendix no.12 p. 750, H.C. 1884–85, (288), ix, 768.

44 Murtagh, *Irish Historic Towns Atlas*, p. 12.

45 *F.J.*, 11 Jan. 1890.

46 *F.J.*, 28 Dec. 1889.

47 Lewis, *A topographical dictionary of Ireland*, i, p. 87.

48 *Commission on market rights and tolls*, p. 327, [C5888], H.C. 1889, xxxviii, 337.

49 *The Westmeath Independent*, 3 Jan. 1857; P.J.Currivan, 'Athlone as a railway centre' in *Journal of the Irish Railway record Society*, iv (1955–7), p. 216.

50 *Royal commission on market rights and tolls: minutes of evidence vol.v*, p. 328, [C5888], H.C. 1889, xxxviii, 338.

51 Sheehan, *South Westmeath farm and folk*, p. 262.

52 *Pigot's directory* 1824, p. 128.

53 Henry Coulter, *The west of Ireland: its existing condition and prospects* (Dublin, 1862), p. 3.

54 Lewis, *A topographical dictionary of Ireland*, i, p. 87.

55 *Parliamentary gazetteer of Ireland* i, p. 96.

56 *Parliamentary gazetteer of Ireland* i, p. 99.

57 Paul M. Kerrigan, 'The Batteries, Athlone' in *Journal of the Old Athlone Society*, i, no. 4 (1974–5), pp 264–70.

58 Lewis, *A topographical dictionary of Ireland*, i, p. 87; P.J. Currivan 'Athlone as a railway centre' in *Journal of the Irish Railway Record Society*, iv (1955–7), p. 210.

59 *Appendix to the second report of the commissioners of Irish education inquiry*, (Parochial Abstracts) pp 776–7, pp 1282–3, H.C. 1826–7, (12), xii.

60 *Royal commission of inquiry primary education (Ireland) vol. vi. educational census. Returns showing the number of children actually present in each primary school on 25 June 1868 . . .* , pp 79, 136, H.C. 1870, [C. 6.v.], xxviii pt. v, 133, 190. (hereafter cited as *Educational census 1868*).

61 Disparate estimates were furnished by the Catholic and Anglican clergy. The religion of the master or mistress shall be used to determine which data from the parochial abstracts should be accepted.

62 *The Athlone Independent*, 1 Jan. 1834.

63 D.H. Akenson, *The Irish education experiment: the national system of education in the nineteenth century* (London, 1970), p. 83.

64 *First Report of the commissioners on public instruction, Ireland*, pp 111a, 112a, 45a, H.C. 1835, xxxiii.

65 *Educational census* 1868, p. 79, p. 136, [C. 6. v], H.C. 1870 vol. xxviii, 133, 190.

66 Westmeath aided applications (N.A. ED 1/89, no. 19).

67 Westmeath aided applications (N.A. ED 1/89, no. 19); *Pigot's directory* 1824, p.129; *F.J.*, 23 April 1831.

68 Roscommon aided applications (N.A. ED 1/76, no. 61).

69 Roscommon aided applications (N.A. ED 1/76, no. 148); Brendan O'Brien, *Athlone workhouse and the famine* (Athlone, 1995), p. 31.

70 Roscommon aided applications (N.A. ED 1/76, no. 148).

71 Michael Quane, 'Athlone Classical School founded by William Handcock and Athlone English School founded by Arthur St. George' in *Journal of the Old Athlone Society*, i, no. 2 (1970–71), p. 97.

72 Akenson, *Irish education experiment*, p. 233.

73 *Dublin Evening Post* 8 July 1857.

74 *F.J.*, 1 Jan. 1878; *F.J*, 31 July 1880.

75 Brother Hubert Cunniffe, 'Our old schools' in *Marist College Annual*, i, (Athlone, 1973), pp 8–20.

76 Michael Quane, 'Ranelagh Endowed School Athlone' in *Journal of the Old Athlone Society*, i (1969), p. 32.

77 Quane, 'Ranelagh Endowed School Athlone', p. 32.

78 *Report of the commissioners appointed to take the census of Ireland for the year 1841* p. xxvi, [504], H.C. 1843, xxiv; *Census of Ireland, 1901 pt ii*, p. 101, [Cd 1190], H.C. 1902, cxxix, 475.

79 *Reports of commissioners on the state of the municipal corporations in Ireland*, p. 136, H.C. 1835, (23), xxvii (hereafter cited as Municipal corporations report).

80 Brendan O'Brien, 'Some aspects of municipal government in Athlone' in M. Keaney and G. O'Brien (eds), *Athlone bridging the centuries* (Mullingar, 1991), p. 80.

81 *Municipal corporations report*, p. 126, H.C. 1835, (23), xxvii.

82 *Municipal corporations report*, p. 128, H.C. 1835, (23), xxvii.

83 Murtagh, 'Tudor, Stuart and Georgian Athlone', p. 340.

84 Lyons, *The Grand Juries of Westmeath*, ii, p. 106.

85 Lewis, *A topographical dictionary of Ireland*, i, p. 87.

86 Murtagh, 'Tudor, Stuart and Georgian Athlone', p. 201.

87 Murtagh, 'Tudor, Stuart and Georgian Athlone', p. 332.

88 Peter Jupp, 'Urban politics in Ireland 1801–1831' in David Harkness, and Mary O'Dowd, (eds.), *The town in Ireland, Historical Studies xiii* (Belfast, 1981), p. 103.

89 Murtagh, 'Tudor, Stuart and Georgian Athlone', p. 341.

90 Walker (ed.), *Parliamentary election results in Ireland, 1801–1922*, p. 197.

91 *Municipal corporations report*, p. 136, H.C. 1835 (23), xxvii.

92 *Municipal corporations report*, p. 126, H.C. 1835 (23), xxvii.

93 *Municipal corporations report*, p. 131, H.C. 1835 (23), xxvii.

94 *Municipal corporations report*, p. 131, H.C. 1835 (23), xxvii.

95 *Municipal corporations report*, p. 136, H.C. 1835, (23), xxvii.

96 *The Athlone Sentinel*, 23 July 1840.

97 *The Athlone Sentinel*, 7 July 1843.

98 Virginia Crossman, *Local government in nineteenth–century Ireland* (Belfast, 1994), p. 66.

99 Crossman, *Local government*, p. 67.

100 Crossman, *Local government*, p. 70.

101 *Report of the Local government and taxation of towns inquiry commission, (Ireland), appendix no. 34*, p. 529, [c1696], H.C. 1877, xxxix, iv, 537, (hereafter cited as *Local government and taxation of towns report*).

102 *F.J.*, 27 Dec. 1850.

103 *F.J.*, 27 Dec. 1850; *Slater's directory 1846*, p. 6.

104 *The Westmeath Independent*, 20 Jan. 1855.

105 *The Athlone Times*, 23 June 1894.

106 *F.J.*, 19 Nov. 1887.

107 *F.J.*, 19 Nov. 1887.

108 Dr Hill to Poor Law Commission office, 21 Aug. 1869, (N.A. C.S.O.R.P. 12798/1869).

109 Dr Hill to Poor Law Commission office, 21 Aug. 1869, (N.A. C.S.O.R.P. 12798/1869).

110 Crossman, *Local government*, p. 71; *The Athlone Times*, 16 Nov. 1895.

111 *F.J.*, 14 Nov. 1891.

112 *Special report by W.P. O'Brien to the Lord Lieutenant upon the local government and taxation of Ireland, made in pursuance of the report of the select committee of the House of Commons dated 20 th. of July 1877 appendix F*, pp. 82–6, [c1965], H.C. 1878, xxiii, 792–6, (hereafter cited as *O'Brien report on local government and taxation*).

113 *O'Brien report on local government and taxation*, pp. 82–6, [c1965], H.C. 1878, xxiii, 792–6.

THE POLITICAL COMMUNITY IN
THE ERA OF O'CONNELL

1 *Parliamentary representation; boundary reports, Ireland*, p. 5, H.C. 1831–2, (519), xliii, 21.

2 Murtagh, 'Tudor, Stuart and Georgian Athlone', p. 332.
3 *F.J.*, 8 Aug. 1830.
4 Walker (ed.), *Parliamentary election results in Ireland, 1801–1922*, pp 195–247.
5 Stephen A. Royle, 'The Lisburn by-elections of 1863' in *Irish Historical Studies*, xxv, no. 99 (May 1987), pp 277–8.
6 Fergus O'Ferrall, 'The emergence of the political community in Longford, 1824–29', in Raymond Gillespie and Gerard Moran (eds), *Longford, essays in county history* (Dublin, 1991), pp 123–51.
7 Peter Jupp, *British and Irish elections, 1784–1831* (Newtown Abbott, 1983), p. 157.
8 Jupp, 'Urban politics in Ireland 1801–1831', p. 106.
9 Jupp, 'Urban politics in Ireland 1801–1831', p. 106.
10 *Parliamentary representation; boundary reports, Ireland*, p. viii–ix, H.C. 1831–2, (519), xliii.
11 *Municipal corporations report*, p. 136, H.C. 1835, (23), xxvii.
12 *Municipal corporations report*, p. 136, H.C. 1835, (23), xxvii.
13 Ann Barry and K. Theodore Hoppen, 'Borough politics in O'Connellite Ireland; the Youghal poll books of 1835 and 1837' in *Journal of the Cork Historical and Archaeological Society*, lxxxiii (1978–9), p. 107.
14 Barry and Hoppen, 'Borough politics in O'Connellite Ireland; the Youghal poll books of 1835 and 1837', p. 107.
15 Walker (ed.), *Parliamentary election results in Ireland, 1801–1922*, p. 197.
16 Jupp, 'Urban politics in Ireland 1801–1831', p. 113.
17 *F.J.*, 23 Feb. 1826.
18 *F.J.*, 31 May 1826; *Dictionary of Athlone biography*, p. 35.

19 *F.J.*, 27 Jan. 1829.
20 *The Athlone Sentinel*, 14 Apr. 1843; *F.J.*, 27 Jan. 1829.
21 *F.J.*, 27 Jan. 1829.
22 *F.J.*, 6 June 1826.
23 *Municipal corporations report*, p. 136, H.C. 1835, (23), xxvii.
24 *Committee on tolls and customs*, pp 61–2, H.C. 1834, (603), xvii, 289–90.
25 *F.J.*, 17 June 1826; Fergus O'Ferrall, *Catholic emancipation: Daniel O'Connell and the birth of Irish democracy* (Dublin, 1985), p. 133.
26 O'Ferrall, *Catholic emancipation*, pp 133–4.
27 O'Ferrall, *Catholic emancipation*, p. 170.
28 *F.J.*, 7 Sept. 1828.
29 *F.J.*, 8 Aug. 1828; *F.J.*, 11 Oct. 1828; *F.J.*, 1 Nov. 1828.
30 Jupp, 'Urban politics in Ireland 1801–1831', p. 120.
31 *F.J.*, 29 Apr. 1830.
32 *Dictionary of Athlone biography*, p. 112, p. 347.
33 *F.J.*, 26 June 1830.
34 *F.J.*, 26 June 1830.
35 *F.J.*, 26 June 1830.
36 *F.J.*, 29 June 1830.
37 *F.J.*, 30 Apr. 1830.
38 *F.J.*, 8 Aug. 1830.
39 *F.J.*, 9 Aug. 1830.
40 *F.J.*, 8 Jan. 1831.
41 *F.J.*, 23 Apr. 1831.
42 *Dictionary of Athlone biography*, pp 390, 154, 254, 149.
43 *Dictionary of Athlone biography*, pp 353, 357, 259, 331.
44 *F.J.*, 16 May 1831.
45 *F.J.*, 6 Dec. 1832.
46 *F.J.*, 19 Dec. 1832.
47 Thomas Hart to Daniel O'Connell, 4 March 1833 in Maurice R. O'Connell (ed.), *The correspondence of Daniel O'Connell* (8 vols, Dublin, 1974), v, p. 13.
48 *The Athlone Independent*, 26 Dec. 1834.

49 *The Athlone Independent*, 31 Dec. 1834.
50 *The Athlone Independent*, 14 Jan. 1835.
51 *F.J.*, 13 Jan. 1835.
52 Brian M. Walker (ed.), *Parliamentary election results in Ireland, 1801–1922* (Dublin, 1978), p. 193.
53 *F.J.*, 10 Oct. 1885.
54 *The Athlone Independent*, 14 Jan. 1835.
55 *The Athlone Sentinel*, 9 Jan. 1835.
56 *The Athlone Sentinel*, 9 Jan. 1835.
57 *Third general report relative to the valuations for poor rates and to the registered elective franchise in Ireland*, p. 187, H.C. 1841, [329], xxiii, 189.
58 *The Athlone Sentinel*, 23 Jan. 1835.
59 Hoppen, *Elections, politics and society in Ireland, 1832–1885*, p. 430.
60 *The Athlone Sentinel*, 9 Jan. 1835; *The Athlone Sentinel*, 21 Jan. 1835.
61 *F.J.*, 29 Jan. 1836.
62 *F.J.*, 16 Sept. 1836.
63 *F.J.*, 16 Sept. 1836.
64 *F.J.*, 7 Apr. 1837.
65 *F.J.*, 4 Aug. 1837.
66 *F.J.*, 19 Jan. 1839.
67 *The Athlone Independent*, 4 June 1841.
68 *The Athlone Independent*, 11 Jan. 1841.
69 *F.J.*, 26 June 1841.
70 *Reports and minutes of evidence taken before select committees on election petitions (Ireland), Athlone election*, p. 68, H.C. 1842, (548), v.
71 *The Athlone Mirror*, 16 Apr. 1842.
72 *The Athlone Sentinel*, 9 July 1841.
73 *F.J.*, 8 July 1841.
74 *F.J.*, 13 July 1841.
75 *Committee on Athlone election petition*, p. 68, H.C. 1842, (548), v.
76 *The Athlone Sentinel*, 9 Jan. 1835.
77 *The Athlone Sentinel*, 9 Jan. 1835.
78 *The Athlone Sentinel*, 31 Mar. 1843; *F.J.*, 3 Apr. 1843.
79 *F.J.*, 31 Mar. 1843.
80 *F.J.*, 7 Apr. 1843.
81 *F.J.*, 14 Apr. 1843.
82 *F.J.*, 7 Apr. 1843.
83 *F.J.*, 3 Apr. 1843.
84 *The Athlone Sentinel*, 7 Apr. 1843.
85 *The Athlone Sentinel*, 7 Apr. 1843.
86 *The Athlone Sentinel*, 7 Apr. 1843.
87 Hoppen, *Elections, politics and society in Ireland, 1832–1885*, p. 391.
88 Hoppen, *Elections, politics and society in Ireland, 1832–1885*, p. 392.
89 *F.J.*, 11 Apr. 1843.
90 *The Athlone Sentinel*, 25 Aug. 1843.
91 *The Athlone Sentinel*, 9 Jan. 1835.
92 *Reports and minutes of evidence taken before select committees on election petitions (Ireland), Athlone election*, p. 24, H.C. 1844, (97), xiv.
93 *Committee on Athlone election petition*, p. 25, H.C. 1844, (97), xiv.
94 *Poor inquiry (Ireland), Appendix D containing baronial examinations relative to earnings of labourers, cottier tenants, employment of women and children, expenditure;and supplement, containing answers to questions 1 to 12, circulated by the commissioners*, p. 31, H.C. 1836, [36], xxxi, 147.
95 *Committee on Athlone election petition*, p. 25, H.C. 1844, (97), xiv.
96 *Committee on Athlone election petition*, p. 17, H.C. 1844, (97), xiv.
97 *The Athlone Sentinel*, 21 Apr. 1843; *F.J.*, 6 Apr. 1843.
98 *The Athlone Sentinel*, 23 June 1843; Brendan O'Brien, 'Athlone's Repeal demonstration', in *Journal of the Old Athlone Society*, i, no 2 (1970–71), pp. 107–11.
99 *The Athlone Sentinel*, 9 Nov. 1838.
100 *F.J.*, 27 Sept. 1842; *The Athlone Sentinel*, 7 Oct. 1842; O'Brien, 'Athlone's Repeal demonstration', pp 107–11.
101 Oliver Mac Donagh, *O'Connell. The life of Daniel O'Connell, 1775–1847* (London, 1995), p. 509.
102 Mac Donagh, *O'Connell*, p. 507.
103 O'Brien, 'Athlone's Repeal demonstration', p. 107.
104 *The Athlone Sentinel*, 19 May 1843.

105 *The Athlone Sentinel*, 23 June 1843.

106 Jacob Venedy, *Ireland and the Irish during the Repeal Year, 1843* (Dublin, 1844), (A.B.L., The Moran Manuscripts, vol. ii, p. 533).

107 Venedy, *Ireland and the Irish during the Repeal Year, 1843*, (A.B.L., The Moran Manuscripts, vol. ii, p. 525).

108 Venedy, *Ireland and the Irish during the Repeal Year, 1843*, (A.B.L., The Moran Manuscripts, vol. ii, p. 533).

109 Venedy, *Ireland and the Irish during the Repeal Year, 1843*, (A.B.L., The Moran Manuscripts, vol. ii, p. 533).

110 Venedy, *Ireland and the Irish during the Repeal Year, 1843*, (A.B.L., The Moran Manuscripts, vol. ii, p. 539).

111 *The Athlone Sentinel*, 23 June 1843.

112 Venedy, *Ireland and the Irish during the Repeal Year, 1843*, (A.B.L., The Moran Manuscripts, vol. ii, p. 542).

113 *F.J.*, 15 Apr. 1845.

114 *F.J.*, 15 Apr. 1845.

115 *F.J.*, 19 June 1844; *F.J.*, 28 July 1845.

POLITICAL DEVELOPMENTS,
1847–85

1 *D.N.B.*, p. 34.

2 T.P. O'Connor *The Parnell movement-with a sketch of Irish parties from 1843* (2nd ed., London, 1886) p. 198.

3 *F.J.*, 30 Mar. 1854.

4 *F.J.*, 30 Mar. 1854.

5 Mary Naughten , 'Judge William Nicholas Keogh' in *Journal of the Galway Archaeological and Historical Society*, xxxix (1981–2), p. 5.

6 *The Athlone Sentinel*, 28 May 1847.

7 *F.J.*, 31 July 1847.

8 *The Westmeath Independent*, 7 Aug. 1847.

9 *The Westmeath Independent*, 7 Aug. 1847; *Slater's Directory* 1846, p. 6.

10 *The Athlone Sentinel*, 6 Aug. 1847.

11 *F.J.*, 6 Aug. 1847.

12 *The Athlone Sentinel*, 6 Aug. 1847.

13 *F.J.*, 10 Oct. 1885.

14 *F.J.*, 30 Oct. 1851.

15 *D.N.B.*, p. 34.

16 Whyte, *The Independent Irish Party*, p. 13.

17 *F.J.*, 9 June 1852.

18 Whyte, *The Independent Irish Party*, pp 59–60.

19 *F.J.*, 12 July 1852; *F.J.*, 21 July 1852.

20 *The Athlone Sentinel*, 7 July 1852.

21 *The Athlone Sentinel*, 7 July 1852.

22 Whyte, *The Independent Irish Party*, p. 97.

23 Whyte, *The Independent Irish Party*, p. 197.

24 *D.N.B.*, p. 34.

25 *The Athlone Sentinel*, 5 Nov. 1851.

26 Naughten, 'Judge William Nicholas Keogh', p. 19.

27 O'Connor, *The Parnell movement*, p. 146.

28 *F.J.*, 11 Jan. 1853.

29 O'Connor, *The Parnell movement*, p. 142.

30 O'Connor, *The Parnell movement*, p. 127.

31 O'Connor, *The Parnell movement*, p. 114.

32 *F.J.*, 30 Mar. 1854.

33 *F.J.*, 30 Mar. 1854.

34 *F.J.*, 18 Jan. 1853.

35 *F.J.*, 22 Apr. 1853.

36 *F.J.*, 30 Mar. 1854.

37 *F.J.*, 30 Mar. 1854.

38 *F.J.*, 30 Mar. 1854.

39 *F.J.*, 23 Apr. 1853.

40 *F.J.*, 23 Apr. 1853.

41 *F.J.*, 21 Apr. 1853; *F.J.*, 23 Apr. 1853.

42 *F.J.*, 23 Apr. 1853.

43 *F.J.*, 5 Mar. 1855.

44 *D.N.B.*, p. 34.

45 *D.N.B.*, p. 34

46 *D.N.B.*, p. 35.

47 *F.J.*, 2 Oct. 1878.

48 *F.J.*, 30 Mar. 1854.

49 O'Connor, *The Parnell movement*, p. 123.

50 O'Connor, *The Parnell movement*, p. 125.

51 Hoppen, *Elections, politics and society in Ireland, 1832–1885*, p. 81.

52 O'Connor, *The Parnell movement*,
    p. 125.
53 Whyte, *The Independent Irish Party*,
    p. 54.
54 *The Athlone Sentinel*, 16 Apr. 1856.
55 *The Athlone Sentinel*, 9 Apr. 1856.
56 *The Athlone Sentinel*, 16 Apr. 1856.
57 *F.J.*, 11 Apr. 1856.
58 *The Athlone Sentinel*, 25 Aug. 1843.
59 *F.J.*, 9 Aug. 1878.
60 Sheehan, *South Westmeath farm and
    folk*, p. 91.
61 *F.J.*, 9 Aug. 1878.
62 *The Athlone Sentinel*, 16 Apr. 1856.
63 *The Athlone Sentinel*, 16 Apr. 1856.
64 *The Athlone Sentinel*, 26 Mar. 1857.
65 *The Athlone Sentinel*, 8 Apr. 1857.
66 *The Athlone Sentinel*, 8 Apr. 1857.
67 Liam Cox, *Moate County Westmeath,
    a history of the town and district*
    (Athlone, 1981), p. 133.
68 *F.J.*, 13 June 1874; *F.J.*, 26 June 1874;
    F.J., 1 July 1874; *F.J.*, 27 Oct. 1874.
69 *The Athlone Sentinel*, 19 Jan. 1859.
70 *The Athlone Sentinel*, 11 May 1859.
71 *The Athlone Sentinel*, 13 Apr. 1859.
72 *The Athlone Sentinel*, 27 Apr. 1859.
73 *Dublin Evening Post*, 7 May 1859;
    Hoppen, *Elections, politics and society
    in Ireland, 1832–1885*, p. 84.
74 *F.J.*, 1 July 1874.
75 *F.J.*, 27 Oct. 1874.
76 *F.J.*, 1 July 1884.
77 *F.J.*, 27 Oct. 1874.
78 *F.J.*, 27 Oct. 1874.
79 *F.J.*, 25 June 1874.
80 *F.J.*, 27 Oct. 1874.
81 *F.J.*, 1 July 1874.
82 *F.J.*, 25 June 1874.
83 *F.J.*, 25 June 1874.
84 *F.J.*, 27 Oct. 1874.
85 *F.J.*, 27 Oct. 1874.
86 *F.J.*, 9 Aug. 1879; *F.J.*, 27 Oct. 1874.
87 *F.J.*, 27 Oct. 1874.
88 R.V. Comerford, *The fenians in
    context* (Dublin, 1985), p. 133.
89 Henry Smith to Inspector General
    of Constabulary, 2 Apr. 1866 (N.A.,
    F 870 1866).
90 Henry Smith to Inspector General
    of Constabulary, 2 Apr. 1866 (N.A.,
    F 870 1866).
91 Henry Smith to Inspector General
    of Constabulary, 26 Feb 1866
    (N.A., F 327 1866); Abstracts of
    cases of persons arrested under the
    Habeas Corpus Suspension Act
    1866, (N.A., CSO ICR 10, p. 138).
92 Henry Smith to Inspector General
    of Constabulary, 26 Feb 1866
    (N.A., F 327 1866).
93 William Beckett to Chief Secretary's
    office Dublin Castle, 1 Feb. 1862
    (N.A., CSORP, 10783/1862).
94 William Beckett to Chief
    Secretary's office Dublin Castle, 1
    Feb. 1862 (N.A., CSORP,
    10783/1862).
95 Comerford, *The fenians in context*,
    p. 125.
96 *The Westmeath Independent*, 9 Mar.
    1865.
97 Copies of information against John
    Mulvey sworn before William
    Beckett R.M., 5 Oct. 1865 (N.A.,
    CSORP, 10504/1865).
98 Abstracts of cases of persons
    arrested under the Habeas Corpus
    Suspension Act 1866, (N.A., CSO
    ICR 11, p. 51).
99 *The Westmeath Independent*, 24 Feb.
    1866.
100 *F.J.*, 26 Sept. 1865.
101 Smith to Inspector General of
    Constabulary, 30 Mar. 1866 (N.A.,
    F 870/1866).
102 Hoppen, *Elections, politics and society
    in Ireland, 1832–1885*, p. 223.
103 Bishop Gillooly of Elphin to Rev.
    F. Murphy, P.P., 1865 (N.L.I.,
    Gillooly Papers Section C).
104 Bishop Gillooly of Elphin to Rev. F.
    Murphy, P.P., 1865 (N.L.I., Gillooly
    Papers Section C); Bishop Kilduff to
    Bishop Gillooly, 5 July 1865 (N.L.I.,
    Gilllooly Papers Section C).
105 *The Westmeath Independent*, 8 July
    1865.

106 Bishop Kilduff to Bishop Gillooly, 5 July 1865 (N.L.I., Gillooly Papers Section C).

107 Bishop Gillooly of Elphin to Rev. M. O'Reilly, P.P., 6 July 1865 (N.L.I., Gillooly Papers Section C).

108 *The Westmeath Independent*, 15 July 1865.

109 *The Westmeath Independent*, 15 July 1865.

110 *The Westmeath Independent*, 22 July 1867.

111 *The Westmeath Independent*, 15 July 1865.

112 Kilduff to Gillooly, c. 10 July 1865 (N.L.I., Gillooly Papers Section C).

113 Kilduff to Gillooly, c. 10 July 1865 (N.L.I., Gillooly Papers Section C).

114 Kilduff to Gillooly, c. 10 July 1865 (N.L.I., Gillooly Papers Section C).

115 *The Westmeath Independent*, 12 Nov. 1854.

116 J. McNamara to Rev. J.W. Hackett, 4 May 1859. (T.C.D., Incorporated Society Papers ms 5805).

117 *The Westmeath Independent*, 22 July 1865.

118 *F.J.*, 10 Oct. 1885.

119 *The Westmeath Independent*, 12 Sept. 1866.

120 David Thornley, *Isaac Butt and Home Rule* (London, 1964), pp 37–45.

121 *The Westmeath Independent*, 19 Sept. 1868.

122 *The Westmeath Independent*, 31 Oct. 1868.

123 *F.J.*, 27 Oct. 1874.

124 *The Westmeath Independent*, 21 Nov. 1868.

125 *The Westmeath Independent*, 21 Nov. 1868.

126 *F.J.*, 25 June 1874.

127 *F.J.*, 20 Nov. 1868.

128 Thornley, *Isaac Butt*, p. 176.

129 *The Westmeath Independent*, 7 Feb. 1874; *F.J.*, 20 Sept. 1873.

130 Thornley, *Isaac Butt*, p. 183; MacDonagh, *O'Connell*, p. 647.

131 *The Westmeath Independent*, 7 Feb. 1874.

132 Thornley, *Isaac Butt*, p. 25.

133 Walker (ed). *Parliamentary election results in Ireland, 1801–1922*, pp 107, 105.

134 Hoppen, *Elections, politics and society in Ireland, 1832–1885*, p. 73.

135 *Special case and judgment in the matter of the Athlone election petition*, p. 1, H.C. 1874, (144), liii, 573.

136 *Athlone election petition*, p. 3, H.C. 1874, (144), liii, 575.

137 *F.J.*, 5 Apr. 1880; *F.J.*, 20 Apr. 1880.

138 *F.J.*, 29 May 1880; *Slater's Directory 1881* p. 332.

139 *F.J.*, 29 May 1880.

140 *F.J.*, 31 May 1880.

141 *Copies of the shorthand writers' notes, not already printed, of all judgements of the election judges*, pp 6–7, H.C. 1880, (337–ll), lvii, 74–5.

142 *F.J.*, 29 May 1880.

143 *The Westmeath Independent*, 27 Mar. 1880.

144 *Judgements of the election judges*, p. 8, H.C. 1880, (337–ll), lvii, 76.

145 *F.J.*, 31 May 1880.

146 *F.J.*, 27 May 1880.

147 Sheehan, *South Westmeath farm and folk*, p. 135.

148 *F.J.*, 8 Nov. 1880.

149 *F.J.*, 8 Nov. 1880.

150 *The Westmeath Independent*, 26 Nov. 1885.

151 *The Westmeath Independent*, 19 Dec. 1885.

152 *F.J.*, 12 Feb. 1881.

153 *F.J.*, 7 Mar. 1881.

154 *The Westmeath Independent*, 8 Apr. 1882.

155 *The Westmeath Independent*, 8 June 1882.

156 *F.J.*, 6 June 1884.

157 *F.J.*, 10 June 1884.

158 *F.J.*, 17 June 1884; Hoppen, *Elections, politics and society in Ireland, 1832–1885*, p. 333.

159 *F.J.*, 3 Oct. 1885.

160 Murtagh, *Irish Historic Towns Atlas*,
      p. 7.
161 O'Connor, *The Parnell movement*,
      p. 126.

CONCLUSION

1   Hoppen, *Elections, politics and society in
     Ireland, 1832–1885*, pp 33–73.
2   Hoppen, *Elections, politics and society in
     Ireland, 1832–1885*, p. 77.
3   *Nation*, 16 Apr. 1859.

4   O'Connor, *The Parnell movement*, p. 126.
5   O'Connor, *The Parnell movement*, p. 126.
6   O'Brien, 'Population, politics and
     society in Cork, 1780–1900', p. 609;
     *Thom's Irish almanac and official
     directory, with the post office Dublin city
     and county directory* (Dublin, 1851), pp
     267–8; *Thom's official directory of the
     United Kingdom of Great Britain and
     Ireland* (Dublin, 1896), pp 1254–7.
7   *Thom's directory*, 1851, pp 267–8;
     Thom's directory, 1896, pp 1254–7.